Myths of Being Human

Myths
of Being
Human

FOUR PATHS TO CONNECT WITH
WHAT MATTERS

BRANDI LUST

ISBN 978-0-9997605-0-5 (softcover)
ISBN 978-0-9997605-1-2 (e-book)

Edited by Andrea Clute
Cover and layout design by Kelley Engelbrecht
Author photograph by Autumn Theodore

To my Grandma Rose. When I was born, I was given your name, and when you died I was given your purpose — to bring love into the world through sharing who I truly am, even when it hurts.

CONTENTS

PATH 4: CONNECTION

Introduction:
Why We Are Here

ARE WE READY FOR ANOTHER WAY TO BE?

Spring, 2013

We are walking down the winding planks that form our path. My hand grips hers, tightly.

"You will be okay," she says.

I nod. Her voice is clear and sure, but the only thing that makes sense to me is the way her fingers clasp mine.

I am shaky. My insides are on high alert; danger is imminent. The world outside is dark, foggy, numb. My body feels small and insignificant.

I am alone. Except for this hand. The only thing reaching me through the dark. Stay focused. *Breathe*.

We keep walking, and eventually find ourselves standing at a waterfall, a place I come to often. We are leaning over the rails, watching the water trickle across the moss-coated rock face.

She squeezes my fingers. *Breathe.*

There are no words for the pain I feel. No way to explain the utter confusion of no longer knowing who I am.

We turn around, and she tells me to keep walking. My sister knows the darkness, and she stays with me there.

I don't know whether I will be okay.

Hours later, when I am home alone, I check my email and find her words.

Bran,

I tried to write you a letter, but it just didn't seem right. I wrote you this. I hope it imparts some reassurance. I love you deeply...I feel as though you are my heart living outside of my body in some ways. I cannot bear to see you so unhappy, mostly because it is clear to me how fine you are and will be. I will tell you as much and as many times as you need to hear it: you will be okay. I am sure of this, with everything I am.

Love,
Your sister

MYTHS OF BEING HUMAN

Hear me deep,
Let my love and words sink into your broken pieces,
You will be okay,
You hold within you everything you need,
You are strong, so much stronger than you at this moment
believe,
I will be your strength if it must live outside yourself for now,
I will always be,
as you are to me…

Please listen, please hear it deep,
I will repeat it as many times as you need,
You are fine,
Everything will be okay,
You have everything within yourself that you could need,
you may feel like the pieces are falling to the ground,
Let me be your gravity,
Let me be your truth,

The pieces are all in place,
Just where they need to be.
They may be uncomfortable,
They're just getting settled,
They will mend,
They will remember their grace,
They will remember that they were whole and realize they were
never out of place…

I am crying tears of relief. I print her words and carry them with me. On a long trip days later, I pack them in my luggage just in case, though I never have to look at them.

The words are a part of me now, sewn into the flesh of my heart. I feel them — the space they take up where once there was only darkness, only panic, only fear.

Spring, 2015

I am standing in front of a room full of people, all staring at me. They are here because they understand brokenness, disconnection, and darkness. They are here because they believe in wholeness, interconnection, and light. I speak their mother tongue.

I am a teacher, and true teachers share their essence with others, hoping to see something reflected back, something that can be held gently, in reverence — because who knows when or how it might be seen again?

Teachers know that this *something* can be cultivated. First by calling it forward, and then by lovingly coaxing it outward, until that *something* in the other person becomes clear enough, becomes apparent enough, even when that teacher no longer exists.

I recognize the light and the darkness in the people in this room. I hold it out between us, let them see who they are and who I am. Together we learn more about what it means to be human.

I breathe, and begin to tell my story.

Reflection

Four years ago began a process of overwhelming, painful upheaval. It started with a decision; I felt it was time to leave my position as a high-school English teacher for something new. After not getting a job in another district, I eventually accepted a role as an instructional coach within my (then) current district.

I loved teaching, and the transition to a different job was difficult. I grieved the loss of my classroom and the relationships I built there. In addition, my new role was isolating; teachers were leary of it and of me. Instructional coaching was a change-agent position, and many were not happy with the numerous changes happening in education — changes which focused on test scores as accountability measures and standardizing classroom instruction. Teachers felt alienated and under-appreciated, and in my new position, I represented the cause of those feelings: an amorphous pressure from above to "be better" in a job that was already quite difficult. I was supposed to still be a fellow teacher, but they weren't so sure. As I began to visit classrooms, they wondered why I was there. Was I judging them? Reporting back what I saw to administration? Did I leave the classroom because

I couldn't handle it anymore? I was spending all my work hours trying to figure out a job that had no clearly defined role, while also facing significant resistance from my colleagues. I hadn't just left a job I'd loved; I'd also stepped into a new one that was both confusing and alienating.

While I was going through this difficult transition, other parts of my life became confusing as well. A friendship I had unknowingly depended on for a long time developed into more serious feelings. I was honest with my husband about those feelings, which was difficult for both of us. In turn, our situation brought to light other issues from our seven-year marriage — issues that almost broke us apart.

Professionally, I felt unsure, ineffective, self-conscious. Personally, I felt ashamed, guilt-ridden, staggered. One of the few people I talked about my personal struggles with was my Grandma Rose. The two of us had always been paired souls. She had taken me into her home for three years as I finished my college degree as a single mother. She would never judge me; in some ways, she *was* me. Throughout her life, intimate relationships were always a struggle for her — a struggle she never quite resolved. While reflecting on her own experiences, she shared challenges and choices that had caused devastation in her life. She also shared wisdom for resilience and patience, urging me to think about all the repercussions of the decisions I made in these pivotal moments.

Then, in the midst of all the other turmoil in my life, it

became clear that Grandma Rose was dying of the cancer that she had lived with for over a decade. Her struggle had been long, yet surprisingly not always arduous; there were even moments when I almost forgot the cancer existed. Always in the corner of my mind, however, was a place I avoided. A part of me that could not begin to imagine what it would be like to live without her — a part filled with anxiety, dread, and sorrow. Now I needed to prepare myself to visit that place and come to terms with the inevitable loss.

Death was at the center of my existence. It felt as though all parts of my life — my identity as a teacher, my marriage and family, and most of all my grandmother — were slipping from my grasp into the ether. For two long years, I lived in this space of nothingness and death.

Clawing my way back to a livable reality required therapy, marriage counseling, a diagnosis of depression and anxiety, and medication. It also necessitated the development of inner resources previously hidden within me.

I turned into myself through the practice of mindfulness and deep reflection. Why or how I made this decision is unclear to me even now. But somehow, I found myself sitting on my bed each evening and closing the door to be with whatever I found in the silence and solitude. Each night sitting, writing, processing, and mourning. Each night seeking and finding even the smallest moments of beauty and joy.

The written words of others, too — poetry, fiction, and spiritual texts — provided solace and a window to look deeper within myself. Pen and paper were my sanity, tools for collecting the wisdom of elders. I filled notebooks that became personal bibles; reading with fury and passion, I transcribed the words of others in my own hand, running my finger back over phrases searchingly. Each book might hold a secret, and I was searching for myself on every page.

When I read back through those journals and notebooks, I see the slow peeling back — layers of ego and identity falling away to reveal something deep, whole, essential. There is no such thing as "the answer," but there is such a thing as the essential self. A truth that is revealed through digging deep, peeling away, finding what's left when everything we depend on to define ourselves falls apart. Finding that self revealed a new and wholly unrealized "me." It revealed a different life, too. Before the tumult was over, I had left my job, applied to graduate school, received a full scholarship, and started my own business.

It's fair to say, however, that at many points in this journey, I had no idea which parts of my life would be left intact. Would I keep my marriage? My job? My sanity? I had no idea. All of the things that made up "me" seemed in flux, totally fluid, and less real than they once were.

As I was going through these experiences, and

particularly the death of my grandma, it became impossible for me to uphold all of the separate selves I had created: work self, wife self, friend self, younger self hiding inside of older self. All of those distinctions fell apart because of the pain I was experiencing, and I displayed the same broken self in all areas of my life. In an effort to find stability, I shared more of my pain with others than ever before, and at the same time, I no longer had the energy to worry about the judgments they might harbor. As I revealed my own vulnerability, others shared more of themselves, too. Bonds of common humanity were created, and deeper relationships were formed. Those relationships were the thread that kept me connected to hope in my worst moments.

I also began to understand the tremendous suffering so many people were facing, not at all unlike my own. Colleagues with mental illness, friends who were struggling in their marriage, family members who had, in desperation, wished there was a way out of this world.

The more I learned, the less alone I felt. In addition, the breaking down of barriers was relieving, even as it humbled me to see the ways I had created so many partial selves in the past. In the months before leaving my position and after having applied and been accepted to seminary as a counseling student, I was asked to write a book chapter targeted to educators. After realizing the common pain so many shared, I wanted to create something that would alleviate suffering, so I designed an action-research project where I would teach mindfulness to educators and administrators I worked with. (That chapter and book were never published, by the way, but the process led me to a vocation that was an extension of my deepest being.)

While facilitating my first workshop, a sense of knowing washed over me. I was still a teacher; this was my work. During the sessions I led, people were finding the same tools that had helped me, and using them to become more complete versions of themselves. I left my job having taught four workshops: Mindfulness, Gratitude, Growth, and Connection. It was a description of my own path, supported by practices and research.

From that point forward, word spread. While the number of participants for these workshops was small, they spoke loudly of the impact. Before I left my school district, my supportive boss suggested that I start a business in order to begin contracting work in the district. She didn't make any promises, but I thought, "Why not?"

And so, organically, I began the work that is still evolving today. It wasn't even in my imagination to do such a thing. And yet, I can see the inklings toward it, the whispers, from the time I was a curious child traced throughout my life. My youthful feeling of "something more" as I walked in nature alone. My teenage obsession with psychology and philosophy. The days I spent as a young adult mourning the suffering of others and wondering what I could do to be present with them. All of this had a place.

Since those first workshops, I have worked in school districts, social justice organizations, universities, and privately owned businesses teaching mindfulness and other tools that reveal our deepest humanity. My work is both an expression of my own personal journey, a developing memoir sprinkled with the poetry of others, and a reflection of the most up-to-date research in the fields of study I work in: mindfulness, gratitude, growth, compassion, connection, resilience, and creativity, among others.

In my own process of discovery, I have looked to researchers, scientists, poets, philosophers, and spiritual teachers as guides; examples of all of these can be found on these pages. While I derive inspiration from a variety of sources, this book is not advocating for a belief system; rather, it is a resource for looking deeper within. When working with organizations, I find that creating an open, inclusive space that allows individuals to have their own experiences and belief systems is important and necessary for common humanity.

This book, much like the rest of my work, is an amalgam of the heart and the head. There are four paths, based upon those first four workshops. Each path will include the poetry of personal experience through vignettes and reflection alongside the supporting science

and practical skills for implementation. Each begins with
a myth upon which I once operated and a reality revealed
through personal experience and supported by research.
Myths are common, false assumptions about how we are
supposed to live, but the realities of our human nature
can free us from struggling to reconcile our lives with
those myths. The paths are:

1. **Mindfulness:** Becoming aware of the present
    moment and accepting it in order to connect with
    reality
2. **Gratitude:** Appreciating positive experiences in order
    to cultivate joyful living
3. **Growth:** Accepting the inevitable difficulties of life
    and allowing them to be transformative tools
4. **Connection:** Recognizing the ways we cannot live
    without one another, and acting though this knowl-
    edge daily

How This Book is Organized

Each path is made of short chapters intended to guide
you through an experience. These will include an introduction to the topic along with a description of the path,
practices, and tools to help you implement it into your life.

Introduction: A statement of myth and a contrasting statement of reality upon which the chapter is based, followed by vignettes and reflections on my own experiences as I struggled against the myth and later embraced the reality.

The Path: Research supporting the new reality: how and why it is true, and what it looks like in action — some food for your left brain.

The Practice: An experiential strategy to be used in daily life. Some of these may be used once a week, some every day. You get to choose how to implement them based on your needs. Practices are evolving and ongoing; they are resources, not exact recipes. You might first try each one as written, then later decide to try something different. Some may work for you, and some may not resonate. The word *practice* itself requires a little context in order to read this book. For the purposes of our journey together, I will use the word *practice* in a variety of ways. You can practice something (verb), but for our purposes, there is also a set of practices (noun), which will refer to ongoing strategies used to achieve specific results. I may also refer to your practice in a broader way, without linking it to one specific tool you might be using at the moment. In this context, I am referring to the evolution of all the tools, strategies, and ways of being that lead to a new way of living in the world. Your practice is *how* you move down the path and through the world.

Tools: These chapters include a starting point, a way to continue, and additional resources to extend your experience with the topic. These are in three categories:

- **Self-Assessment:** Self-assessments are your starting point. They help you to further explore where you are right now. They may include quizzes you can access online and prompts for journaling.

- **Intentions:** For our purposes, an intention is a personal statement you use as a reminder of the path you would like to follow. Intentions are based upon your personalized goal and are a way to connect with your values. A word about goals and intentions: they are the most helpful if they are subject to modification. It's good to keep in mind what's important to you, but not to grip it too tightly. In this way, the vision for the future doesn't close down new perspectives and insights, or other ways of seeing things.

- **Mentors:** Mentors are extension resources. You may seek additional support outside of this text. These sections provide experienced guides you can turn to for help and ways to keep exploring. This being said, this book is intended to be an experiential process. Engage the chapter by doing, and then go back and see where you would like to learn more.

Supplementary Online Resources

In addition to the text sections of the book, there are supplementary resources available online which you may find helpful. For example, there are worksheets and videos for some of the practices. There are also links to all of the resources mentioned in the text (including the Self-Assessment Tools and some of the Mentors' resources). For access to any of these items, go to the password-protected page:

www.brandilust.com/book-resources

Once on the page, enter the password *myths*. You will have to enter this password each time you use the page. There is a short introductory video you may choose to watch. If you want to use the other practice-based videos (which you may return to more frequently), you can also access these by going to brandilust.com and viewing the "Videos" page.

Throughout the text, I will refer you to www.brandilust.com/book-resources in order to use optional supplementary materials. While not mandatory, these may be quite helpful. In addition, for the Self-Assessments and Mentors sections and any other resources mentioned in the text, the supplementary page is a convenient way to access all items quickly and easily.

Please take a few moments and visit www.brandilust. com/book-resources and enter the password *myths* so that you can become familiar with the resources available there. Please also visit brandilust.com and view the "Videos" page. You may want to bookmark both of these pages for easy access while reading.

How to Use This Book

This book is set up like a training series I facilitate; it is intended to provide an eight-week program. If you choose to use the text in this way, your schedule will look something like this:

- **Week 1,** Focus on Mindfulness: Read Path 1, take the self-assessment, determine your intentions, and begin the practices.
- **Week 2,** Focus on Mindfulness: Continue with your intentions and practices.
- **Week 3,** Focus on Gratitude: Read Path 2, take the self-assessment, determine your intentions, and begin the practices.
- **Week 4,** Focus on Gratitude: Continue with your

intentions and practices.

- **Week 5,** Focus on Growth: Read Path 3, take the self-assessment, determine your intentions, and begin the practices.
- **Week 6,** Focus on Growth: Continue with your intentions and practices.
- **Week 7,** Focus on Connection: Read Path 4, take the self-assessment, determine your intentions, and begin the practices.
- **Week 8,** Focus on Connection: Continue with your intentions and practices.

At the end of eight weeks, read the Conclusion, which focuses on maintaining an ongoing engagement with the skills, strategies, and mindsets created throughout the eight-week process. In addition, in order for certain brain changes to take place, formal mindfulness practice should continue throughout the entire eight-week period (and beyond, throughout the rest of your life — I hope). If you want to get the absolute most out of this book, this is what I recommend. (There is a weekly checklist in the Supplemental Resource section of the book which you can use if you follow this program. In addition, there is a worksheet you can download on the Book Resources page, www.brandilust.com/book-resources.)

Another suggestion for getting the most out of this resource is to find a small group of people you would like to go through the process with. Meet with these folks every week or two to discuss the topic, reflect on the practices, share insights, and process difficulties. A group process can help you learn much that is not written here; it does for me every time I facilitate. As an additional benefit, using the book in this way also incorporates accountability, which is a change-facilitation tool; we are more likely to do things when others know we are doing them and when there are specific deadlines others depend on. If you are interested in starting a Myths discussion group, please use the Facilitation Guide, which you can sign up for on the website www.brandilust.com.

So what will you gain from engaging this process? Let me share what it has done for me. Four years ago, I did not know I was suffering. However, I carried with me a constant, nagging sense that there was always something slipping through my fingers. I had a gnawing urge to do more and more in order to elicit whatever was missing. This sense pushed me to pursue achievements, and I was praised for attaining them. Society loves go-getters, doers, and perfectionists. Fitting into these norms won me superficial rewards. However, no matter what words of affirmation I received, no matter what new finish line I crossed, it was always the same. Inwardly, I knew something was broken or wrong; I just didn't know how to fix it.

At the same time, I was protective of my inner world,

even of its existential dread. If people saw this "wrongness" within me, the illusion of my success might be broken. I created walls between myself and the world unknowingly, and instead of sharing what was inside, I built a facade based upon what I perceived others valued most about me.

This inauthenticity was unsustainable. I lashed out because I felt my needs weren't being met in my relationships and circumstances. And how could they be? I wasn't even being honest with myself about what I needed. This frustration mounted over many years, and it seeped into my most important personal connections, poisoning what intimacy and comfort I may have found in them.

As things started to fall apart for me through my relationship problems, unhappiness in my work, and the death of a loved one, the facade on which I had depended fell apart — at first slowly, then faster and faster. In the end, I was left with nothing but myself, the most essential me. The fog from my depression, anxiety, dread, and deep grief eventually cleared, and I had another chance to figure out who I really was and what I wanted from life. This chance was possible because I engaged the four paths shared with you in this book. I learned how to be present in my own life through mindfulness. I remembered to be grateful for beauty and joy despite the pain. I made meaning from my difficulties and transformed them into opportunities for growth. And, most of all, I reached out to those around me and found belonging, community, and love.

The life I live now is one of integrity and truth. It is still not easy, but it is real and wholesome. I am a better wife, mother, and friend than I have ever been. My relationships with others are deeper, and my compassion is more expansive. In my work, the authenticity and empathy I've gained lead to rewarding, fulfilling collaborations and networks of people who know I will bring my whole self to everything I do. They trust me. I also trust myself. I have flaws, but at the same time, there is a deep and abiding belief in my own ability to make the right decision, to see things through, to know what is called for in this moment.

I am still growing, and my life is still in flux. Only a year after leaving my job to go back to school, I left a scholarship and an amazing educational community to do this work. However, when that time came, and I once again needed to leave a place where I felt at home, I knew it was the right choice. I trusted myself and did the hard work of following my inner voice, even though that meant disappointing people I cared about and leaving good opportunities behind. I had learned how to create a life that is my own, and these seeming drawbacks didn't stop me from following my own truth.

The clarity I feel now comes from authenticity, a

quality that improves my own life and also helps me to improve the lives of others. I bring my flawed, human self to everything I do; this has been the most important shift in my personal journey, as well as my professional work. Through telling my story and sharing the tools that helped me grow from darkness into a more sustaining life, I now help others to do the same. This has led me to believe that if each of us chooses to be more present, to recognize joys, to learn from sorrows, and to connect more deeply with one another, it is not only our personal lives and experiences that will improve, but also our workplaces, our communities, and our world.

A culture that doesn't embrace imperfection or emphasize common humanity in all aspects of life — personal relationships and professional work — encourages the creation of false selves that are ultimately dehumanizing. Our culture often denies the importance of authenticity in public life (and especially in the workplace), but instead focuses on meeting outcomes — whether that is profit in the case of businesses, test scores in schools, number of followers on social media, or perceptions of others in almost every facet of public life.

But what would it look like to change this culture? I am fortunate enough to explore this question in my work. Initially, I partnered with organizations that wanted to enhance employees' personal well-being and improve their stress management. Along the way, I began to see, and then to consciously facilitate, larger changes within the culture of organizations — changes which fostered authenticity and humanity. Individuals began to bring their whole selves to all of life, personally and professionally. Consequently, they cared more deeply for one another, and they became better team members.

The *Myths of Being Human* refers to shifts in individual thinking, but also to these larger, cultural shifts. Our collective consciousness is focused more on cognition than on presence, more on getting what we want than on loving what we have, more on chasing happiness than on accepting reality, and more on individual outcomes than on interpersonal connections. The question is not whether these myths are good or bad, but whether they are life-giving or life-negating. This book is an argument that there are other ways to view the reality, and that a shift in individual perspective can lead to larger shifts that ripple out into the world we inhabit.

If any of this rings true for you, then please read on as I tell my story, share some tools, and try to provide a little of the wisdom I sought and found on all the pages that have come before these.

MYTHS OF BEING HUMAN

Path 1: Mindfulness

STOP LETTING YOUR THOUGHTS
RULE YOUR LIFE

myth #1

Humans are primarily
thinking beings.

---

reality #1

Humans are experiencing,
feeling beings who are
also able to think.

CHAPTER 1

Introduction to Mindfulness

Spring, 2012

It's the end of another school year. I've just given my high-school students an anonymous survey about the class, something I always do around this time. After collecting the responses, I quickly flip through them, my hands shaking slightly. Ninety percent of the reviews are positive, sometimes even touching. The other 10% contain some phrase, sentence, or sentiment that turns my stomach and sends a wave of heat through my body.

At the end of the day, I separate my surveys into piles. I take out the ones that tell me I am sometimes a pushover, or confusing, or difficult. I read them over and over, feeling worse each time.

My internal dialogue has full control at this point. I spend the next days wondering whether I should even be in the field of education. My thoughts and feelings unfold into long conversations with colleagues in which they try to reassure me of my worth as an educator:

"You started X new program."
"You connected with X student."

Nothing they say resonates, because no success can counteract the internal voice telling me I'm worthless. My value comes from being successful in every single thing I do, and I'm not. I'm a failure.

But I *am* happy, right? If not, the only possible reason would be that I am selfish, unable to be satisfied. I have two healthy children, an attentive and kind husband, and personally meaningful work as an educator. And yet, I continually strive for "something more" I can't quite identify. There is a place within me that is never quite touched by the successes that I've been fortunate enough to experience. A single negative comment can send me crashing into an ocean of self-loathing.

Spring, 2013

I am crying in my car on the way to work, as I do many mornings. I have trouble sleeping now, and eating seems nearly impossible. My thinking is foggy, I've lost 10 pounds, and I frequently feel like I need a glass of wine.

How did I get here? I am totally disconnected in my marriage, which is on the verge of ending. My husband thinks I might be sick. I have started smoking again years after having quit, and I am definitely drinking too much. My new job as an instructional coach has left me lonely and isolated, and worst of all, my Grandma Rose, my soulmate, is dying.

If I wasn't worthwhile before, I am practically useless now. Something must be wrong with me. The once-subtle whisper of the "something more" that's been missing has become an alarm.

"You're broken," the voice inside my head tells me.

I believe it.

Spring, 2014

My oldest son, Jory, is up in his room studying. I have just tucked my four-year-old son, Sawyer, into bed for the night, and my husband, Jamey, is downstairs folding laundry. Alone, I enter my dark bedroom, quietly shut the door, and light a candle before settling onto the floor and shutting my eyes. I can hear the pattering of rain and smell the scent of wet earth coming through the cracked window beside me. I breathe. I remember that I am breathing. I try to feel the cool air flowing in, the warm air flowing out.

Sometimes I get swept up in a feeling, or a thought carries me away:

I need to remember to make that appointment.
I think I will tell Jamey to...
I can probably make this better by...

And yet, I try over and over to return to the sensations of each breath. Even when everything in me wants to get off the cushion, leave the room, move away.

And sometimes it saves me, too — this space I have created. The solitude, the silence, the peace, are all things I crave.

I can never tell how my ritual will go, but every night I try again.

Spring, 2015

I am walking along the bank of a river with my husband and five-year-old son. I have recently taught my first mindfulness workshop to a group of educators in my school district. A man in the group shared how he began noticing the pattern of bark on the trees as he took his daily walks, something he had never been aware of before our work together. It made him feel grateful, he said.

His words echo in my mind as I walk along the edge

of a forest next to the river and then sit down on a fallen log, examining closely the moss-covered cracks and touching the peeling skin of the tree closest to me. I can feel the whorls and crevices of the rough bark and the spongy pliancy of the bright green moss growing on top. I close my eyes and inhale deeply. Inside, I am still and quiet. I feel grateful.

"What are you telling that tree, Momma Mia?" Sawyer questions, calling me by my family nickname.

"I'm telling the tree it's beautiful," I say after a moment's thought.

He promptly comes to where I sit and begins lovingly caressing the bark of the same tree. (This is the son who tells me I am beautiful, hand to my cheek, almost every day.)

We literally hug the tree together. Then, via his prompting, planning, and subsequent stick gathering, we begin tapping out a rhythm on its trunk with two fallen branches that, in his words, "tell the tree it's beautiful, and we love it."

Reflection

The shift I experienced over these years was an adjustment of awareness and attention. It was a long, strenuous journey moving from the place where I lived inside my head, a slave to my own self-talk, to a place where I was able to engage in the world around me with curiosity. It began in 2014 when I reconnected with a practice I had learned from my Grandma Rose many years before. This time period was tumultuous, to say the least. In addition to the many life circumstances I was facing — new job, death of a loved one, marriage difficulty — I had also recently experienced my first major depressive episode (though at the time I was yet to be diagnosed).

I didn't call the practice I was doing mindfulness at first; I called it meditation. My New-Age Grandma Rose had had her own meditative practice for as long as I could remember. On the nights I stayed with her as a little girl, I spent most mornings playing quietly with the amethysts and crystals on the table of her lavender meditation room while she sat across from me on the floor silently, eyes closed. That same room became my bedroom when I came to live with her as a nineteen-year-old with a toddler son.

When I was five, these actions of hers were strange to me. Then and for a long time after, I knew no one else like Grandma. Twenty-seven years later, only a year and a half before she died, I was now doing the same thing, and it was saving me.

Meditation, or formal mindfulness practice as I call it in my work, is part of the healing process I adopted at that time and continue to practice today. Formal mindfulness practice is a secular version of meditation. While meditative, or contemplative, practice has roots in many faith traditions, and mindfulness in particular is based upon practices often used in the Buddhist tradition, formal mindfulness can be used by those of any or no faith tradition. It is, in essence, a brain-change activity. This being said, I often hear from those I work with who do have a faith path that mindfulness enriches the belief system they have chosen. While this is not the specific goal of the work I do with others, I am glad they have found deeper meaning in that area as well.

Mindfulness is much more than just meditation, however, which is only one tool used to hone our awareness and attention. Mindfulness, generally, is a conscious combination of ways of thinking and techniques that help us be present in the moment, this moment, as in the only one that truly exists for us.

Some people talk about the present as the "infinite now." I usually explain it to people in this way: no one, not a single person in the world, can determine what is going to happen 30 seconds from now. You could take this book and throw it across the room. You could decide to set it down and take a nap. No one knows — not even you. Furthermore, we never have true recollection of the past. Each time we relive a memory, it is a less-accurate re-creation. When you consider all of this, it becomes much clearer that the present moment is all we can count on.

And yet, people spend a large percentage of their time reliving things that have already happened or pondering future possibilities. Mindfulness helps bring this reality into awareness and offers other options for experiencing the world.

CHAPTER 2

The Path Toward Mindfulness

Our brain is a complex system of neural pathways. Like babbling streams and rushing rivers, these pathways are built upon the course of our every thought, memory, and insight. Each time we engage in a mental process, the currents of that path grow stronger, and the banks are washed into deeper and wider channels, making it easier for thoughts to flow.

So which tributaries do we give our energy to, and are they leading us to the places we want to go? My neural pathways were once fast-flowing rivers swelled with thoughts of worthlessness and perfectionism. I was always working hard to be "better," and when that was disrupted by any criticism from others, this quickly flowed into self-blame, sometimes followed by depression. I would try to counter these feelings through seeking continual affirmation from others. When that didn't work, my next step would sometimes be to hide from the negative feelings through numbing. This might include alcohol, television, cigarettes, or some other quick fix.

For all of us, this process of building the contours and tributaries of the brain begins in early childhood, for better or worse. In the introduction to *Bouncing Back: Rewiring Your Brain for Maximum Resilience and Well-Being*, Linda Graham states, "Whether we tend to bounce back from terrible setbacks or stay where we've been thrown depends on learned patterns of response to others and events. These patterns become fixed, not just incorporated into a behavioral repertoire but deeply encoded in our neural circuitry, from an early age."

Somewhere in my early years, my way of coping became to expect perfection and then mentally attack myself when I didn't deliver. Because these systems and patterns were so ingrained, they likely would not have changed without conscious and targeted effort. Using mindfulness as a tool, however, I am reshaping the landscape of my brain.

Our brains are incredibly powerful; they control our reality for better or worse. And yet, there is little cultural or educational focus on cultivating the brain into a space where we would want to be. Brains do much more than think, but it is our inward thoughts, and particularly our self-talk, that we give so much of our attention to. If our brain tells us, "You need to go faster," we do. If it says, "You sucked in that meeting," we believe it. In *The Untethered Soul: The Journey Beyond Yourself*, author Michael Singer aptly states that if we were to take the voice in our minds and imagine him or her as a person sitting beside us, that person would hardly be someone we would trust or value as a confidant. With constant contradictory sentiments and continual reminders of our less-admirable characteristics, we would probably dislike that person intensely, in fact. And yet, we trust our minds to guide our every decision, and we invest our emotions in the stories they tell.

Through my mindfulness practice, I started conditioning my brain to be present with current experiences instead of investing so much energy into the past, the future, and the stories in my head. I stopped connecting my thoughts so deeply with my identity, and I began identifying more with other parts of my experience. I also grew the pathways of patience and kindness. If my mind wandered, I gently pulled my attention back, even as it sometimes evoked frustration or discomfort to do so. This gave me some peace and objectivity in my daily life that had been impossible before. Now I can begin to choose which rivers will run dry and which streams will become the major waterways of thought and active response. We all have this capacity.

The reality is that our brains are much more than instruments for self-talk, reliving the past, and pondering the future. They are also instrumental in connecting us with our bodies, which are rich sources of information, experience, and feeling. Neuroscientist Antonio Damasio believes that emotions arise as experiences in the body that are then interpreted by the mind. Demasio has also done research that shows how these emotions are key to our ability to function normally. When studying patients with damage to the brain's emotional regulators, Demasio found individuals were unable to make simple decisions, such as which restaurant to visit that evening. While we consider decision-making a mostly rational activity, this study and others like it show that our emotions are critical to this process. It becomes incredibly difficult to make even the smallest of decisions, such as choosing a restaurant, without them.

The process of cultivating moment-to-moment awareness begins when we notice sensations: the touch of skin against skin, the smell of rain in the air. It continues as we explore experiences within the body that occur as a result of things happening in our environment: the tightening of the stomach before a difficult encounter, or the rush of tingling warmth when someone we care about expresses affection. Connecting with our direct experience also includes awareness of the many emotions these sensations and experiences evoke — euphoria, grief, calm — which are all mental interpretations of the stimuli we encounter. Mindfulness is a way to become aware of these other ways of being: we notice sensations in the body as well as the emotions evoked by those sensations. This greater awareness leads to modes of experiencing and knowing the world that are not separate from the mind, but are certainly distinct from conscious thought.

Without attention and awareness (which can be developed through mindfulness) the more subtle but important landscape of our physical sensations and emotional responses can get swept out of our consciousness by the directive and noisy space of our minds. We get carried away by ruminating on the past and the future and lost in running narrative, even when other ways of knowing — emotions and sensations, for example — are equally valid.

A note here about thinking: it is not the enemy. Thinking is an amazing ability; it can help us to be rational and compassionate. In mindfulness practice, we don't need to prevent thoughts from happening. We simply gain more practice connecting with other parts of our experience, too, while also creating distance from our thoughts in order to increase objectivity.

In the long run, my personal goal for mindfulness practice is to change the types of thinking I do. For example, due to my own practice, I can sometimes go days without hearing one single negative thought about myself. However, that doesn't mean I've stopped thinking. In fact, my thoughts are more helpful and clear. Mindfulness practice has improved my thinking; it is now a tool for understanding as opposed to a single perception of reality.

Connecting with emotions, sensations, and experiences happening in the moment can also make us happier. Psychologist and happiness researcher Matt Killingsworth conducted one of the world's largest studies on human happiness through trackyourhappiness.org. He collected data from over 15,000 people in order to study how "mind wandering" affects happiness. (Mind wandering is thinking about something other than what's happening right now.) Through text messages, he asked three questions: *How do you feel? What are you doing? Are you thinking about something other than what you are doing?* The third question was the largest predictor of happiness, even when individuals noted in the follow-up questions that they were thinking about something pleasant. His study also found that the average person spends 47% of their time in a mind-wandering state, leaving us present in the moment only about half the time. This leaves much room for improvement and growth.

Mindfulness practice is one tool to increase the percentage of time we spend in the present. Its effectiveness depends upon the brain's inherent ability to change throughout the human lifespan. This capability is referred to as *neuroplasticity*. Professor of Cognitive Neuroscience at the Institute of Cognitive Neuroscience University College London Sarah-Jayne Blakemore defines neuroplasticity as "the ability of the brain to adapt to changing environmental stimuli" (as cited in Storr, 2015). This adaptation can be positive or negative, but the more we engage in a particular thought or behavior, the more hardwired that thought or behavior becomes. Mindfulness practice works because of what Blakemore describes as "experience-dependent" plasticity. This type of plasticity occurs throughout life as a response to learning and environmental changes such as those that mindfulness provides.

Through neuroplasticity, mindfulness literally changes the structure of the brain. Neuroscientist and Harvard professor Sara Lazar has studied some of these changes. In a 2005 study, Lazar and her team analyzed long-time practitioners of Insight Meditation (which focuses attention on internal experiences). Using an MRI scanner, they found these practitioners had increased cortical thickness in parts of the brain associated with "sensory, cognitive and emotional processing" compared to a control group. Later, in a 2011 study, Lazar and her team expanded these findings. In this second longitudinal study, participants underwent two MRI scans, one before and one after an eight-week mindfulness-based program. When compared to a control group who did not participate in the eight-week program over the same time period, the mindfulness-trained participants had increased gray matter in brain areas associated with "learning and memory processes, emotion regulation, self-referential processing, and perspective taking." These changes took place with participants practicing, on average, around 30 minutes daily.

Studies like these show many research-based benefits associated with mindfulness practices, which are increasingly gaining attention as a helpful intervention in a variety of settings within therapy, social work, education, and business. The benefits of mindfulness for therapy clients includes: reduced rumination on the past and future, reduced stress and anxiety, improved working memory, increased ability to focus, increased cognitive flexibility, higher relationship satisfaction, improved overall well-being, increased empathy, and reduced psychological distress. In addition, the *State of the Science: Implicit Bias Review 2016 Edition* included mindfulness-based interventions as a tool for mitigating the effects of implicit bias[1] in education and other work settings, citing a number of promising studies.

---

1 Implicit bias is defined in the *State of Science: Implicit Bias Review* 2016 Edition as "The attitudes or stereotypes that affect our understanding, actions, and decisions in an unconscious manner. Activated involuntarily, without awareness or intentional control. Can be either positive or negative. Everyone is susceptible."

MINDFULNESS

We exist in paradox. Our natural human tendency is to live in our minds for almost half of our lives, despite the fact that connecting with our direct experience — getting outside our own thoughts — enlivens our humanity and creates many personal benefits. Through practice, individuals can choose to consciously strengthen specific pathways so that our brains have direct experience more often. Mindfulness practice takes place "on the cushion." It also takes place off the cushion as we choose to come back to the current moment over and over again: when we remember that we are breathing, and feel the lungs releasing air; when we connect with our bodies and remember to feel our feet, planting us to the earth. These things are available every moment; we need only to become aware of them.

In either practice, on the cushion or off, there are two main components of mindfulness: awareness and acceptance. Awareness is conscious attention to whatever is unfolding in the moment internally and externally. Acceptance is the ability to be aware without judgment, accepting all that is unfolding compassionately.

In my personal experience and in my work with others, these two life skills never reach a point of completion. Some experiences are easier to accept than others; some circumstances naturally lead to distraction from the moment. Becoming mindful is a lifelong process. Of the two components, I see people struggle the most with acceptance, and in particular, self-acceptance. It is part of many people's experience to feel as though there is something within them that is inherently wrong, broken, or bad.

This is why it's so important that formal mindfulness practice not become another thing that's done to be "good" or "better," because this implies that there is a "bad" to begin with that needs to be fixed. If a person engages in formal mindfulness practice and spends all of their time telling themselves that they are terrible at it, then the practice is worse than useless. It's perpetuating the very thing it should be helping to resolve: our sense that we aren't good enough as we are, right now.

CHAPTER 3

Mindfulness Practices

FORMAL MINDFULNESS, OR MINDFULNESS "ON THE CUSHION"

Time Commitment: 10–15 minutes

Frequency: Daily for the next eight weeks (and hopefully for the rest of your life)

Resources: A timer, notebook to use as a journal, and a pen or pencil

Optional Online Resources: Mindfulness Practice Log, Five-Minute Breath-Focused Practice Video, and Ten-Minute Breath-Focused Practice Video

As previously stated, mindfulness is a continual state of being, not just a practice. However, mindfulness "on the cushion" has many physical, psychological, and emotional benefits. Primarily, it facilitates brain change, or neuroplasticity. A person engaged in formal mindfulness practice chooses compassionate connection to the moment over and over, strengthening the ability to do this in other contexts. For this reason, it is one of the most important things I do in my own life.

I find it is often difficult for people I work with to commit to this practice regularly. I think this is because it takes time every day, and it is not always fun. Without it, however, it's more difficult to reap the benefits of neuroplasticity. You can "get it" that thoughts don't have to have power over you, but still act in ways that aren't true to this understanding. Formal mindfulness practice gives you the skills to distance yourself from your thoughts by practicing over and over.

It's best to start small: try a 5-minute breath-focused practice (directions to follow and video link available on the Book Resources page) followed by a few minutes of reflection through journaling each day. As you build this habit and reap the benefits, you may decide to sit for longer and use the 10-minute video. Before that happens, accomplishing goals to build on will give you confidence to continue. As you reap benefits and feel more committed, you may want to increase your practice even more to

20–30 minutes. That's up to you, however.

Starting in this way is also helpful because it incorporates reflection, which is incredibly important for learning; in some ways, reflection *is* learning, at least learning that is personally meaningful. It allows you to name what has occurred so that you can replicate successes and avoid what hasn't worked in the past. While writing isn't easy for everyone, it is powerful and worthwhile. My advice is to journal for two weeks, then go back and read what you wrote. You will see why it is vital.

Your main goal as you begin is to create a habit, which is more powerful than relying upon personal motivation every day. You won't always be motivated, but once a habit is established, it takes far less willpower to complete a task; motivation becomes less of a barrier. If this metaphor helps, think of your brain as a muscle, and formal mindfulness practice as exercise. You keep your body healthy by flexing and using your muscles (even when you don't feel like it). You keep your brain healthy through formal mindfulness practice, which also changes the physical structure of the brain. It's the same principle.

Lastly, I always tell people that even if you don't start now, this information will be there when you need it. I came to mindfulness because I was in a dark place in my life; I needed something different. If you get to this place, it will always be available.

There are many, many tools for engaging with

mindfulness practice (see *Mentors* on page 69) but here are the basics of a simple breath-focused practice:

1. **Posture and Place:** Find a quiet place to sit either on the ground or in a chair. If you are in a chair, make sure that all four corners of your feet are planted firmly on the ground, and your arms are in an open posture, hands resting on thighs or knees. If you are on the ground, you may want to sit on a pillow for comfort. It's best if your seat is elevated above your knees. Once you have found a sitting position that works for you, imagine that there is a string attaching the top of your head to the ceiling (or sky). I tell people they can imagine this string and sway their body slightly under it to begin; this keeps you relaxed but also steady and upright. I suggest setting a timer for your practice, beginning with 5 to 10 minutes.

2. **Become Aware of Your Breath:** Bring your awareness to your breathing. Don't simply notice that you are breathing, but instead connect with how it feels to breathe. Become aware of how your nostrils feel alternately warm and then cool. Become aware of how your lungs feel, expanding and then contracting. Become aware of how your abdomen feels, rising and falling gently. Then, wherever the sensation of breathing is most prevalent for you, rest your awareness

there, lightly.

3. **Accept Your Experiences:** As you try to stay connected to the sensations of breathing, you will notice thoughts and feelings. Know that this is okay, normal, and nothing you need to change. Just gently bring your awareness back to your breathing over and over. If it helps, you can use a technique described by Sharon Salzberg. Imagine your thoughts as clouds in the sky. They are present, but they float through your experiences. You don't have to invest in your thoughts; simply let them pass. This same process can be used for emotions: you notice them, but they don't consume you. Above all, remember to be gentle with yourself, no matter what you experience. There is no right or wrong way to think or feel. You are simply being present with whatever unfolds.

Before moving forward in the book, please feel free to set a timer and take 5–10 minutes for your first practice now. After you have some experience with breath-focused awareness, you can also alternate with other types of mindfulness practice. One of these is walking mindfully. Mindful walking builds your capacity for silence and your ability to be fully with your experiences. However, it moves the focus of awareness from your breathing to all of the sensations that come from walking, and in particular, the feeling of your feet on the ground as you move. One benefit of this practice is that you can do it while also engaging with the natural world. (More on this later with the Shinrin Yoku practice.)

For those beginning this practice, I like to dispel the myth that it is going to turn any person into someone without negative emotions. You aren't going to suddenly stop feeling angry or sad. You will still have days where you do or say things you regret out of an emotional response. Mindfulness practice is about becoming aware of whatever is unfolding now in a generous and empathetic way. This gives you choices. In the words of Victor Frankl[2], "Between a stimulus and a response there is a space. In that space is your power to choose your response. In your response lies your growth and freedom." Mindfulness practice simply gives you more space.

My morning routine is a good illustration of the benefits of cultivating this space. At this stage in our family, my seventeen-year-old now drives himself to school, but my seven-year-old, Sawyer, comes with me each morning. My job from 7:00 a.m. to 8:00 a.m. is to make sure that Sawyer and I make it to school on time with all of the

---

2 While this quote is often attributed to Victor Frankl, I found additional, contradictory information on the Victor Frankl Institute website. It states that this quote is Stephen Covey's *interpretation* of Victor Frankl's perspective, but it is from a book which Covey did not actually cite in his work.

requisite things having been done: we have eaten breakfast, we have brushed our teeth, and we are wearing clean clothes. (This last one is surprisingly difficult, as Sawyer loves to pull dirty clothes out of his hamper so he can wear the same thing each day; sometimes I catch this in time, sometimes not.) Every morning we do these same things, yet every morning I find myself repeating the list over and over again, only to come back and find that Sawyer is doing something totally different, like building a home for his stuffed animals out of Legos.

When this stimulus arises in my environment, I have various physical sensations: a quivering in my stomach, a slight shakiness in my hands. These feelings are a physiological response, and the emotions we sometimes ascribe to them are anger or frustration. When I feel these sensations labeled *frustration*, it may stimulate interpretations, such as thoughts. I may think:

Really?! Did he truly "forget" what I told him to do ten times already? That's impossible.

Or

He literally ignores everything I tell him! He has no respect for my parental authority. I've lost all control.

These thoughts may enhance my physiological response, increasing my emotions as the story I tell myself builds.

Or, I may notice my physiological response and the interpretations that followed. I may then choose not to invest my mental energy into a story about what his internal world is like, but instead focus on a solution. If I choose to do this, I may come up with a more creative way of dealing with the problem, such as using a timer and telling him how long he has to do the items I have assigned him. I might write the list down and give it to him to look at, so I don't have to keep saying the same things over and over, and he can build self-sufficiency.

Before mindfulness practice, I wasn't aware that I had this choice, and I would often act out of my sensations, emotions, and thoughts immediately. This resulted in yelling, anger, and general crazy-making on my part, which was often the cause of escalation and hectic mornings. Now that I know I have a choice, I may decide to express my anger, or more and more often, I may choose not to. This choice comes from my practice. Of course, I still get frustrated, and sometimes I still escalate situations when I wish I wouldn't have. However, I can say these things happen less frequently than they used to, and this is progress.

Overcoming Obstacles to Developing Your Own Mindfulness Practice

While most people I work with understand on a cognitive level that formal mindfulness practice will benefit them, this still leaves the challenge of actually doing it. Much like beginning a workout routine or a healthy eating regimen, while many people aspire to sit each day, a much smaller percentage of people actually follow through and create that habit. I want to help you avoid some of the self-talk that could prevent you from getting on the cushion, while also providing some advice on how to best get started.

There are two major excuses I hear for why people don't engage with their own practice once they leave training with me. The first is that they don't have enough time. I heard this even from people who were committed to the process, so I did a little investigating, and realized people were expressing scarcity thinking. Scarcity thinking often occurs when there is a real or perceived shortage of an important resource; it limits long-term thinking in favor of short-term benefits. The phenomenon has been studied via the effects of poverty on the brain by researcher and Harvard Economics Professor Sendhil Mullainathan and his colleagues. In a 2013 study, they found correlations between diminished cognitive performance and economic hardship. Scarcity literally changes our brain functioning for the worse.

These findings can be generalized to scarcity in *any* important resource, including time. We live in a culture of time scarcity; it is considered admirable to be too busy to think straight. It is the norm to have daily calendars filled with more tasks than we can possibly accomplish. This culture, and our individual behaviors, lead to an outlook that values short-term gains over long-term benefits, which ultimately leads to a lower quality of life. Knowing this can help you to make better choices, even when your brain tells you you shouldn't. Formal mindfulness practice will be one of those choices.

The second obstacle I frequently hear is that taking "self time" feels selfish and falls low on the priority list for many people. However, while mindfulness practice may be for you, too, it is also for everyone around you. Dan Harris, news anchor and author of *10% Happier: How I Tamed the Voice in My Head, Reduced Stress Without Losing My Edge, and Found Self-Help That Actually Works*, narrates a funny video called "Why Mindfulness is a Superpower: An Animation." In the beginning of the video, a mouse driving a car gets cut off in traffic. He proceeds to experience a range of physical sensations and thoughts that bring him to the conclusion, "I'm pissed." In reaction to this, he jumps out of the car and chases down the offender in a rage; it's then that you see in the backseat his little mouse babies who have been watching the whole time.

Who is hurt in this scenario? In the long run, the offended father mouse may certainly be embarrassed. He may also have a negative encounter with the other driver that could ruin his day. Perhaps more concerning, his children witness the inappropriate behavior, are likely to model it, and may even be victims of their father's surplus anger later. How many of us have been angry or emotional about something totally unrelated to our loved ones, but have been unable to control acting out against those we love the most? We can improve this. I have seen it in my own life. Mindfulness practice trains us to take space between a stimulus and a response, and it enhances our ability to do this in everyday life.

My suggestion is to plan an intervention for yourself when either of these excuses arise.

When you hear, "I don't have enough time to practice mindfulness," say to yourself,

I am operating from scarcity thinking, and I am going to make a choice that will benefit my overall quality of life instead.

When you hear, "Taking time for me is selfish and I should be doing _____," say to yourself,

If I practice mindfulness regularly, I will be better for everyone else around me, and especially for those I love the most.

REJUVENATION MAPS

Time Commitment: 20 minutes

Frequency: You will create the map only once, but you will use the rejuvenation points on the map as needed.

Resources: A piece of paper and pen or pencil

Optional Online Resource: Stress Ladder Worksheet

We all have moments in daily life that make us feel alive and present. These experiences help us to cope, especially in times of stress, so I call them rejuvenation points. Rejuvenation points contrast with other coping mechanisms we may use to numb present experience, such as binge-watching television or drinking alcohol to escape negative feelings. While there is nothing wrong with having a beer or watching a favorite show, if they become a habitual escape from unpleasant experiences, then they are doing more harm than good. Ultimately, we are inhibiting our own ability to build resilience and diminishing our ability to connect with others, which is especially important in times of stress (more about this in Section 4 on connection).

This being said, we need to have time and tools to recuperate and recharge, or we are no good for anyone.

Rejuvenation Maps are one tool I use to help people identify healthy and life-giving ways to cope. These maps are also guidelines for the activities and moments in which you are naturally more mindful. Consequently, engaging these experiences more frequently can create a happier life.

Instructions to Make a Rejuvenation Map

Grab a paper and a writing utensil. Fold the paper in half so that there are two sides. On the left side, write "Outer Quiet." These are experiences where you are in a silent, or at least quiet, setting. Make a list of these moments. Here are some of mine: working from home (without music), walking to pick up Sawyer from school, during formal mindfulness practice, when hiking or walking in the neighborhood, in the library, at an art museum.

Now fold the paper out. On the blank half of the paper, write "Inner Quiet." Inner Quiet has three qualities:

1. **You experience less "mind wandering."** As a reminder, this term comes from Matt Killingsworth's research on happiness, and it refers to any time you are thinking about something other than what you are doing.

2. **You have fewer or slower thoughts.** While it's rare to have no thoughts, inner quiet means that the thoughts you do have are less intrusive.

3. **You are more connected with your physical sensations.** Sights, sounds, smells, taste, and touch are more apparent. Your senses are engaged in moment-to-moment experiences; you are aware of your feelings and your environment.

Look back at the first side of the paper, and indicate whether you are **also** experiencing inner quiet when you are experiencing outer quiet. Do this with a phrase such as: *always, frequently, sometimes, rarely,* or *never.*

Here is an example.

Outer Quiet	Inner Quiet
Working from home (without music)	rarely
Walking to pick up Sawyer from kindergarten	sometimes
During formal mindfulness practice	sometimes
When hiking	frequently
At an art museum	frequently
In a library	frequently

Circle the "outer quiet" items on the list where you frequently experience inner quiet as well. For me, these items would include: hiking, visiting an art museum, and going to the library. These circled phrases are the beginnings of a personal Rejuvenation Map, a map of healthy ways to recharge.

So reflecting even further, are there other times when you experience inner quiet, but your environment is not quiet at the same time? For example, during yoga there are often verbal instructions and sometimes gentle music, but inwardly, I have fewer thoughts and am more sensation-focused. If you have times like this, add these additional items to the Inner Quiet side of the paper where you have extra room. Here is what I added to my own map: during yoga, while dancing, when *attentively* listening to another person, when creating art or sometimes when writing, while snuggling with my kids, or when playing with my dog.

This third list provides more options for rejuvenation and additional variety. Maybe you need to recharge, but don't feel like being alone. If you were me, a good option might be to engage in a meaningful conversation or go dancing with friends, for example. You will have your own favored activities.

As a final note, these maps are wonderful for group discussion. Through sharing your maps and hearing from others, you and the rest of your group can leave with some new rejuvenation points to try.

Creating Interventions

When you have finished your Rejuvenation Map, spend some time reflecting on how you manage stress. We all have what I call *stress tells*, which are clues that we are feeling overwhelmed and are not on a road to wellness. I put these into four categories: thoughts, sensations, emotions, and behaviors. Below is a chart that maps my stress tells during low, medium, and high levels of stress. "Low" stress refers to the beginning signs of stress, whereas you also have a default level or baseline where you feel generally capable and can manage the challenges you encounter without feeling detrimental effects.

Stress level	Thoughts	Sensations	Emotions	Behaviors
Low	I need more time. How will I get this all done? I want to sleep.	Fast thoughts Shaky hands Tiredness Less hungry	Tense Frustrated Rushed Self-conscious	More likely to break work/home boundaries Check social media and email more frequently

Medium	How can I make this better?	Queasy	Anxious	Less present with family
		Little appetite	Fearful	
	I need to be careful.	Sugar cravings		Let go of some self-care routines and possibly engage in some unhealthy coping mechanisms
High	Will I be okay? Am I crazy?	Stomach in knots	Depressed	Significant weight loss
			Emotional	
	How will I get through this?	Exhausted but unable to rest	Hopeless	Little to no self-care
		Physically ill	Disconnected	Panic attacks
		Frequent desire to cry		

In order to create this map, I first determined three life circumstances where I experienced some stress (low), quite a bit of stress (medium), and overwhelming stress (high). For each, I tried to evoke the thoughts, emotions, sensations, and behaviors experienced at that time in my life and write them down. Not surprisingly, patterns emerged. As I continued up what I describe as my *stress ladder*, physical and emotional symptoms became more difficult to manage, and simultaneously, I did a worse job of taking care of myself.

Take a few moments to write down the ways you react in times of stress and consider using the Stress Ladder worksheet to help you organize your thoughts. These are your stress tells. Keep in mind that while there may be similarities to my own ladder in your responses, every person reacts to stress and challenges differently, so your stress tells are going to be unique to you.

Now go back and consider your Rejuvenation Map. What on your map could be used as a replacement behavior or a "treatment" for some of these stress tells? Choose a lower-level stress tell, and write an intervention. Hopefully, if you intervene early, you can avoid the high-level tells that come further up the ladder. Here is a framework you can use:

When I experience _____ *(insert stress tell) I will* _____ *(insert something from your Rejuvenation Map).*

So, for example,

When I experience the urge to check social media more frequently than I would like, I will go take a walk outside.

In addition to "treatment" for intervention purposes, this map can also be used as a preventative measure. There are some things on my map I do daily to keep my mental and physical health in order and stay happy — I practice yoga, play with my dog, and spend time with my kids. In times of higher stress, however, I try to do more. Maybe

I go on a long walk in a public park or make sure to call a close friend and talk. These are interventions that I know will help me keep from engaging in more negative coping mechanisms.

As you begin to use your Rejuvenation Map, keep a reflective log to see what works best for you, and when. In addition, you can share your intervention statement with someone else to increase accountability. You can also post it where you will see it regularly as a reminder.

A final note on rejuvenation maps, stress ladders, and creating interventions — none of this is magic, and it truly is about taking the time to figure out what works for you. Even when you do, there will probably still be moments when you feel overwhelmed and don't cope well; I know there are for me. However, what I can promise is that if you use these tools consistently, your overall quality of life will improve, and while things will still be difficult at times, you will recover more quickly and easily from the difficulties. That has been my experience and the experience of those I have worked with.

SHINRIN YOKU

Time Commitment: 20 minutes

Frequency: Once in the next two weeks, and then as desired after

Resources: A wooded area

Shinrin Yoku, otherwise known as "forest bathing," originated in Japan, where it is considered a therapeutic intervention that helps with mental and physical health. It consists of walking through the woods while immersed in sensory experience.

There are a number of physical and mental health benefits of this and similar activities. Time in nature and natural settings is associated with physical health benefits, such as lower blood pressure and enhanced immune-system functioning. Nature is also a mood and energy booster and can help to restore focus in times of stress.

In accordance with Attention Restoration Theory as described by psychology professor Stephen Kaplan, nature also promotes attention recovery. Restorative factors, such as our perception of natural environments as an escape from our normative setting and the "soft fascination" natural elements hold for us, have therapeutic benefits on our attention. An example of such a natural element might be the slow-moving ripples of water created by a fallen leaf. It's an interesting stimulus, but also calming and subtle, as opposed to the stimulus of an action film, which may be enthralling but can also be overwhelming.

Shinrin Yoku can be facilitated by a guide, but it can also be done as an informal practice while walking alone or in a small group. Here are some guidelines:

1. **Turn off your cell phone.** Eliminate all possible technological distractions.

2. **Walk slowly and deliberately.** Feel your feet as they connect with the ground beneath you.

3. **Maintain silence.** Listen.

4. **Bring awareness to the senses.** Notice smells, sensations, colors, shadows, and all the other stimuli in your environment.

5. **Pause.** Be still. Take your time. Touch things. Look closer.

These are the basic instructions. There are also many activities that can be used individually or in groups to enrich the experience. When leading Shinrin Yoku walks, I have used many of the practices in the 40-page guide available for download at Shinrin-Yoku.org. It is a valuable resource I highly recommend.

CHAPTER 4:

Tools for Mindfulness

TOOL 1: SELF-ASSESSMENT

Self-awareness is one of many benefits of mindfulness practice, and a key skill I try to facilitate in my work with others. In order to begin the process of increasing your self-awareness, complete the short form of the "Five Facet Mindfulness Questionnaire" available through the American Mindfulness Research Association. As a reminder, you can find this and all self-assessments at brandilust.com/book-resources; use the password *myths* to enter the page. The five facets measured on this questionnaire are: maintaining nonreactivity to inner experience, acting with awareness, having the ability to observe, being able to describe, and experiencing non-judgment of inner experience.

After you have taken the assessment, reflect on your results through a five-minute free write. A free write is a "stream of consciousness" form of writing where you attempt to keep your pen or pencil moving on paper for a set amount of time without stopping, not putting too much thought into what you want to express. Questions you may ask yourself to start your free write include:

- Did you think your scores were accurate? Why or why not?
- What new information did you learn about yourself?
- Based upon this assessment, what meaningful change might come from having a mindfulness practice?

As you engage in this reflection, if you find yourself feeling judgmental, maybe think of this quiz as a starting point, and maintain an attitude of "not yet."

I have not yet established the skill of consistently acting with awareness, but I will build it over time, for example.

TOOL 2: SETTING AN INTENTION

As a reminder, an intention is a personal statement used as a reminder of the path you would like to follow. Intentions are powerful, because whatever we are aware of and give our attention to grows. A simple example of this is the shift in thinking when you have a recent change in your life, such as getting a dog. With this outward life change, your inner awareness changes, too. You notice things you might not have noticed before: stories about dogs, other dog owners, pet talk at work — all of this becomes fodder for increased attention and awareness. You may also start to see the world a little differently, a little more puppy-like. For example, while walking, you may think, "Man, my dog would go crazy over this." Increased awareness and attention has shifted your worldview. This happens in daily life without conscious effort. With a tool like an intention, increased awareness and purposeful attention is cultivated in order to have a specific, desired effect.

All of this being said, silence is one key aspect of mindfulness; it is what creates the "space" between the stimulus and response. Silence is also counterculture. How often do you sit in a group of people without someone in the room talking? How many seconds can you pause before responding to a question that has been asked?

In order to build comfort with quiet and pause, set an intention to notice where you find silence in daily life for the next week; remind yourself of this intention in the mornings and at any point throughout the day that you remember. At the end of each evening, reflect in writing on where you found silence, and how those silences affected you.

At first, you may notice that you don't have much silence, and that is okay. I have heard from many people that as they engage in sitting mindfulness practice, their capacity and appetite for quiet grows. It becomes a fulfilling part of their life to have a break from the constant noise we encounter throughout most of our days.

TOOL 3: CONNECTING WITH MENTORS

There are many people who do an excellent job of explaining and guiding people through building a mindfulness practice, and sometimes it takes hearing these concepts a number of ways until you find the one that is right for you. Here are some other resources I recommend if you want to keep learning about mindfulness and its benefits:

Tara Brach's podcast, *Tara Brach*. In this podcast, author, psychologist, and mindfulness teacher Tara Brach gives a dharma talk (or Buddhist teaching) combined with mindfulness practices. Topics she covers include forgiveness, self-acceptance, compassion, and building a mindful presence. I listen to this podcast when I need to recenter.

Sharon Salzberg's book *Real Happiness: The Power of Meditation: A 28-Day Program.* In this book and audio CD, author Sharon Salzberg guides participants through a month of mindfulness that includes breath-focused awareness, mindful walking, body scans, and loving-kindness practice (more on some of these later). I have recommended this resource to a number of people who have attended my mindfulness workshops and retreats, and have received positive feedback.

Dan Siegel's book *Mindsight.* Dan Siegel is a UCLA School of Medicine clinical professor of psychiatry who explores brain change in his research and his writing. I had the pleasure of listening to a lecture by Dan Siegel, and that experience evolved the ways I think about mindfulness and brain change. This book provides more insights into the science behind the practice.

Path 2: Gratitude

LOVE THE ONE YOU'RE WITH

myth #2

Humans are satisfied when they have
what they want.

---

reality #2

Humans will never be satisfied unless
they love what they have.

CHAPTER 5

Introduction to Gratitude

Summer, 1988

I am six years old — a small, imaginative child, wide-eyed and dreamy. My feet are bare; pebbles and dirt crumble under my toes as I walk the old dusty track where my father once rode his childhood pony bareback. The grass and wildflowers grow tall around the path, broken from the bright blue sky by rolling hills. My thoughts meander as I stroll, watching bees and small, white butterflies flit among the goldenrod.

Home. The word feels warm and safe. I am welcomed here.

In offering, I put out my hand and silently urge a fluttering creature to rest on my palm. One lands gently on a fingertip, and I smile, whispering, "Thank you."

Summer, 1998

I am sixteen, resting in a crack in the earth. Appalachian mountains swell around me as my hand dips slowly in and out of still water. I hear friends' laughter in the distance, whooping and splashing, but I relish a feeling of peaceful solitude.

This moment...and this one...now another. Each passing second unfolding like waves, subtle and sweet.

I will remember this. This moment, happening over and over again. "Thank you, thank you, thank you," the words come each time, as easy as a breath.

Winter, 2012

It's Saturday morning, 6:00 a.m. The cell phone on my night stand is simultaneously buzzing and vibrating, a cacophony intended to jolt me out of slumber.

I roll over on my back, groaning loudly. It's time to get Jory up to make the team bus for his wrestling meet. I will myself to move, but habit is stronger than motivation. Jamey gets out of bed to take him while I lie there, wallowing in discontent and chastising myself for laziness.

By 8:00 a.m., we will all be bracing ourselves against the cold and scraping the frost from car windows to drive an hour outside of town for his meet. We will sit on hard bleachers for 6 to 8 hours or longer in a gym that smells like my 15-year-old son after lifting. Mysteriously, my body will ache from lack of movement (a dichotomy I will never understand). Then we will drive another hour back home with precious little daylight dwindling away through the rearview window. By the end of the day, I will have spent six straight days in a school building between my job and wrestling meets. This will leave me approximately 36 hours of free time (including sleeping), some of which will be taken up by grocery shopping.

These are the things I tell myself in my wallowing. The rest of the day plays out similarly; I fight against each moment, willing it to be different. While sitting on the bleachers, I imagine how I could be laying down on a soft couch where my legs might ache less. When we are five hours into the meet, I fantasize about enjoying the outside air on a brisk walk. I am fiercely aware of the dwindling reserves of unstructured time available to me, and resentful of my commitments on a moment-to-moment basis.

36 hours, now 35, now 34, my mental clock keeps track in the background as I begrudgingly remain in the now.

Winter, 2014

I am in my bedroom alone, door closed. A candle burns, and the lamplight is low. On my lap is a journal with moments collected over the months — joy, connection, love, and beauty captured in sentences on each page.

I put my pencil to paper and begin to write: "Jory's smile as he teases me before walking out the door, the soft feeling of Sawyer's fingers as he pulls me down the side-walk on the way to school, seeing the light bend through the trees and feeling it warm me from the cool morning chill, Brushing my lips to his cheek and the pleasurable squeeze I give his small body before he leaves for the school building, Hearing joyful, nonsensical chatter of children as they greet one another and seeing the faces of parents as they walk away, still thinking of their own little people…"

Micro-moments of joy. I capture them all, live them again, feel the warmth of remembering.

Winter, 2015

It's Saturday morning, 6:00 a.m. Jamey's tablet rings in the bed, waking us both, and I groan softly. As is his habit, he gets up first and lets our puppy Tucker out to go to the bathroom before waking up Jory to catch the bus for his wrestling meet.

PATH 2: GRATITUDE

I am still resting listlessly under the covers when he comes back into the bedroom and playfully drops Tuck on top of me. "Good morning, Tuck," I say sleepily as Jamey continues about his morning routine. He says goodbye to the two of us, still snuggling in bed when he leaves the house with Jory, and then I finally force myself up and rouse Sawyer for breakfast.

By 8:00 a.m., we are heading to my favorite local market for doughnuts. I am texting my parents that we will come to the wrestling meet bearing gifts. We get to the high-school gymnasium after exchanging many hugs and joking together in the wintery cold of the parking lot. Then we sip hot coffee and share a bag of doughnuts while we all catch up on the bleachers. Within the hour, Jory comes to greet us and tells us he is up next.

When he takes the mat, I reflexively hold onto my mom's shoulder and grit my teeth as my dad laughs at my theatrics. While I have never gotten used to seeing my son in positions that seem both painful and dangerous, I have developed a deep respect for his grit and determination — working out for hours a day, carefully monitoring his weight, putting himself on the mat over and over, even after losing tough battles.

The match begins, and I am swept up in my desire to see his hard work pay off. "Alright Jory! Let's go!" I yell over and over.

My mom is a renowned cheerleader, and I often tell

the story of how she was the only person to ever cheer for my husband's corporate softball team when she came to one of his games. This time, however, she is joined by many voices. Jory has the largest cheering section on his team: both of my parents, Jamey, Sawyer, and me, plus Jory's dad Lyon and his son Gunnar.

I hear the echo of my own excitement, my father's laughter as he puts his arm around me in an affectionate embrace. I feel the hot coffee warming my hands, and the rumble of the bleachers as people pass. I see my son's look of determination and my mother's warm smile as she sits with my six-year-old curled on her lap. These people, all the people I love most, are here in this room. We are cheering for my son as he does what he loves.

Can I be anything but grateful?

Reflection

Gratitude. The word does not encompass the sense of wonder that should be a natural response to the life I have been given in this fleeting moment. The gift to feel, right now, the cold chill of metal under my palm as I type these words, the soft, downy surface of my slippers as I wriggle my toes. To hear the chatter of my seven-year-old as he excitedly cheers for his avatar in a video game and to look out my window to see frosty white snow on the last shivering leaves of fall. These things are not a given; they are a gift of being a living, breathing human who happens to exist in this specific moment which will never happen again.

This world, being alive in it, is magic. Throughout my life, I have fallen in and out of this understanding, but I have never stopped believing it. Some of my most vivid memories of my youth are steeped in a feeling of awe, and whether I touch and experience that same sense in the current moment, I have always known it exists.

However, as an adult, it feels easy, and maybe even natural, to fall into materialism and get weighed down by life's many responsibilities. When this happened to me, it looked like impatience. I had so many things to do that were keeping me from the chance to experience what made me feel alive. All the while, I was forgetting that the only chance I had to experience that feeling at all was to do so in this moment, right now.

In the last few years of my adult life, however, I came to the realization that while I can't will a sense of awe and wonder, cultivating gratitude creates an opening that makes these feelings more likely. My own daily gratitude practice began when I took time alone at the end of each day to reflect on what little gifts had been given to me. In the long run, I named this practice Beautiful Moments. This reflection ultimately changed my everyday experience outside of the few moments I spent journaling. The good things in my life no longer got swept away in the wash of daily experience. I now had a record of all the many joys in mundane living.

I also became more grateful, wonder-filled, and awe-struck generally. When I settle into the moment and look around with new eyes, I now find there are so many nuanced and worthwhile details to savor.

Due to this practice and others, gratitude has increased my well-being. I am more joyful and at peace, simply because it feels better to be alive each day. I have more patience for the mundane because I am no longer seeking to change the experience I am having. My life is richer and more fulfilling.

CHAPTER 6

The Path Toward Gratitude

Anyone can cultivate gratitude, and there are many practices that can facilitate greater awareness of the joy that already exists for us. Mindfulness, just being present in the moment for whatever is unfolding, is one. Another is cultivating our ability to notice goodness. Through reflecting upon positive experiences, which strengthens the neural patterns that create positive experiences in general, we enhance this ability. This has the benefit of cultivating joy, and it also fortifies resilience. If we are able to notice the small, positive occurrences in the mundane, these moments can sustain hopefulness even in dark times.

Robert Emmons is a professor of psychology at the University of California, Davis and a well-recognized expert in the study of gratitude. He defines gratitude as a two-stage process. The first stage is the recognition "that there are good things in the world, gifts and benefits we've received." The second stage is locating the sources of good as outside of ourselves. The sources might be other people, society, the time and place one was born, or even a higher power — whatever that means for the individual. Gratitude practice includes:

- Relishing good experiences in daily life
- Recognizing life challenges as opportunities for growth
- Understanding the many ways each of us have lives of fortune that could have been different (for example, living in a time and place where medical treatment improves the outcome for many diseases while others at different times and places in human history have not had this luxury)

Building on these characteristics and definitions, gratitude is more than saying "thank you." It is also more than recognizing when something exceptional happens and appreciating it. Gratitude is about cultivating awe for the everyday human experience — the good and the bad.

Due to evolution, however, our minds have a natural inclination to pay more attention, for longer, to negative stimuli than to positive ones. This is most likely because awareness of threats better allowed the human species to survive in times when physical dangers (such as predators) were far more likely than today. This negativity bias, or unconscious focus on the negative, influences the way we view others, how we interpret events, and how we see the world. We unconsciously operate through this wiring without realizing we are doing so. Furthermore, society exacerbates our negativity bias through continual focus on negative events and the darker aspects of human interactions in local and national media sources. This only compounds the bias we already have naturally.

If we can consciously replace this bias with a deeper awareness of the positive experiences and opportunities available, however, we will change our perceptions of reality, and therefore our lives.

Part of this process is letting go of the urge to, in the words of research professor Brené Brown, "dress rehearse tragedy." Thinking about the myriad ways that things can go wrong — or holding back from fully engaging in joyful moments for fear of when those moments will end — robs us of appreciation and gratitude.

Gratitude and appreciation can counteract our fear-based negativity bias, lower our stress levels, and help us appreciate the moment by reframing negative experiences and emphasizing positive ones. Experiencing awe at one's daily existence is both an extremely simple idea as well as a difficult practice, however. On one hand, there are millions of moments and gifts for which we can each be grateful every day, from the smile on a loved one's face to living in a time and place where we can travel quickly for work or fun. At the same time, it is so easy to dismiss the mundane and lose touch with the fact that existence is a gift — a transient gift. Biologically, we are programmed to see the extremes and dismiss the normal.

There are many benefits of enhancing gratitude. One study by gratitude researchers Robert Emmons from the University of California, Davis and Michael McCollough from the University of Miami tracked gratitude journaling compared to other types of journaling over three separate studies to find the effects of a more grateful life-perspective. They found self-reported increases in happiness and optimism for those who used gratitude journals. Having a gratitude practice was also shown to have physical health benefits such as better sleep quality and reduced stress. Other emotional benefits correlated with gratitude include greater subjective well-being and reduced anxiety and depression. Perhaps most interestingly, gratitude can enhance our ability to relate with others (which has many physical and emotional benefits in and of itself). Interpersonal benefits associated with being more grateful include closer relationships and increased compassion and altruism.

Research shows that there are simple gratitude interventions, and that these interventions could help us to achieve greater well-being, a higher quality of life, and improved relationships. With only five minutes daily, you may begin to reap some of these benefits.

CHAPTER 7

Gratitude Practices

BEAUTIFUL MOMENTS

Time Commitment: 5 minutes

Frequency: Daily for the next two weeks, and as desired afterward

Resources: Journaling notebook and pen or pencil

Additional Considerations: You can combine this practice with your formal mindfulness practice, even using the same notebook, and spend a few minutes before or after sitting to write down your beautiful moments from the day.

PATH 2: GRATITUDE

Awareness is a powerful tool. It determines our reality — because wherever it is directed, that area of life grows, and becomes more apparent to us. Beautiful Moments is a practice intended to direct awareness toward the pleasant, joyful experiences in life through continued reflection and re-creation of sensory experience. It is a brain-change activity that can be used daily (or even more frequently if you carry a small notebook). It looks like this:

1. **Sit down with a notebook and a pen or pencil.** Reflect on the last 24 hours. When did you experience joy or positive sensations, even if they were fleeting?

2. **When you remember a moment, spend some time recalling all of the sensory details, and write them out as you remember them.** What did you see? Smell? Hear? Feel? Be as specific as possible. This doesn't have to be in complete sentences; it can be a list of phrases, words, bullet points, or even sketches. The goal is to recreate the experience for yourself, internally, as clearly as possible.

3. **Continue this process for as many moments as come to mind.**

Having these moments written down provides an excellent resource for finding objectivity and beauty in difficult times and remembering what is most important every day. When my life is hard, I can look back through these moments, remember the positive, and cultivate gratitude. In addition, patterns evolve over time that allow me to build a more meaningful life. For example, many of my moments are related to nature, even just a sunrise on the way to work. After noting this development, I take advantage of the outdoors more often as a way to enhance joy and to recover from challenges. My go-to for when I need to recuperate is as inexpensive and accessible as a long walk in my own neighborhood.

The Beautiful Moments practice evolved from a gratitude journal I began keeping after I encountered the benefits of thankfulness in my research. When I first started, my entries were merely lists of things for which I was grateful, like this:

I am thankful for blue skies full of clouds, starry nights, full moons, morning haze, beautiful sunrises, tears, poignant songs, perfect words.
— Dec. 2014

I found that these lists were sometimes redundant. In addition, as I continued to research, I realized that engaging the full range of sensory information through reflection would utilize and strengthen more neural pathways for positive experience. Eventually, I transitioned to a more descriptive and specific form of journaling. For example:

Beautiful moments: watching the cloud-swirled sun peeking through blue and white in a fuzzy haze, noticing the interwoven roots of a riverside tree tangle on the banks and reach to the water, feeling the cool breeze brush over my skin leaving tingles, seeing a teacher love in the face of a difficult student.
— Mar. 2015

I share this specific form of gratitude journaling with others in my workshops, along with the opportunity to reflect on where participants find beautiful moments in their own lives. Hearing these joyful vignettes from others is one of my favorite parts of what I do. Each story becomes part of my own experience, a bit of common humanity I carry with me. If you can find others to start the practice with, you can enhance your own joy through these positive interpersonal experiences, too.

SAY IT OUT LOUD

Time Commitment: 5 minutes

Frequency: Once in the next two weeks, then as desired.

Resources: None

Most people I work with are generally grateful for those around them. However, I find a common pattern many of us share is that we feel these things, but are less likely to let others know. "They know how I feel," we might say. But do they? Would we ever want to leave this in doubt?

My friend Mel said this best when she told me about her frustrations with the words "more than you will ever know." "Why don't they know?" she asked. "We should be doing everything in our power to make sure that people know how much we love them, how much they mean to us, what we appreciate about them."

I have caught myself, more than once, using these seemingly loving words to try and express what someone means to me. Mel is right, however. Sharing how we feel about others, with even the smallest of gestures, enhances relationships and spreads happiness. How many overlooked moments of comfort, pleasure, or inspiration have each of us experienced because of the actions of another? Think about the last time someone thanked you for something small. How did it feel? What effect did it have? For me, these moments are little treasures.

So the practice is this: find a way to thank someone who has brought value or joy to your life. This might be as simple as a phone call or a thank-you card. You may even shoot a quick email or text. The mode doesn't matter. What does matter, however, is being as specific as possible. Praise that provides detail is more meaningful to the receiver.

As an example, if someone tells me, "I really enjoyed your workshop. Thank you," that, of course, is pleasant to hear. However, if someone gives me a specific example of how working with me helped them, then it means so much more.

In one of my first workshops, I had a woman who shared such an experience with me, and it is one I still think about to this day. I will call her Margaret. Margaret was at a happy hour with a couple of colleagues after work, and she and another woman were both ready to leave. As they walked out together, Margaret's friend was talking rapidly, complaining about something frustrating she was experiencing in her job. When they got outside, Margaret looked up and noticed that the sun was setting, and the sunset was quite beautiful. She grabbed her friend by the shoulders and turned her toward the sky so that she could see, too. Her friend just stopped talking, and they stared at the colors together and hugged each other. Margaret shared how this experience would never have happened if she hadn't come to my workshops, because she wouldn't have been paying attention the way she was in that moment.

While this interaction happened years ago, I can still recall all the details as if it were my own story. Knowing that I contributed to a moment of connection and joy for Margaret and her friend still brings me warmth and pleasure. This is the power of specificity.

RECOGNIZING AND CONNECTING WITH OTHERS' SUFFERING

Time Commitment: 24 hours

Frequency: Once in the next two weeks, and as desired afterward

Resources: None

One way to recognize the good is to see the many alternatives through the eyes of others. Imagine what it might have felt like on the coldest days of winter to sleep on a sidewalk instead of a warm home. Recall the many who have lost (or never had) the ability to walk on two legs under their own power or run playfully in the park with children. These situations are the reality for many people in the world.

While it may seem morbid, connecting with others' suffering is a way to cultivate profound gratitude for what you have. This is different than feeling guilty. Instead, it's about being deeply, profoundly appreciative. I have sometimes struggled with the guilt I feel for my great fortune.

However, I also try to remember that recognizing and appreciating my many gifts is also honoring those who go without. For example, I could take for granted the running water and indoor plumbing in my home, accept it as a given and barely even notice it's there; this is a perspective of great privilege. Or, I can remember that having drinkable water is a luxury. I can remind myself of the incredible convenience and pleasure of not having to go outside in the middle of the night to use the restroom. This is a much more humble perspective that also pays homage to others less fortunate.

The practice is this: choose one "gift," or a daily experience that's important to you, and try to imagine your life without it. As you do this, connect with the understanding that there are people in the world who are going without that gift and living the very situation you are imagining. Then, over the next 24 hours, notice when you are reaping the benefits of this gift, and give thanks.

The gift you choose to appreciate in this way can be a material convenience or a psychological convenience. For example, you may choose to give thanks for indoor plumbing, running water, food, clothing, access to information, or medical care. However, you could also choose to direct your awareness to the psychological resources many go without: comfort from loved ones, belief in yourself, trusting relationships, or a perception of reality that is confirmed by others around you.

Each time you are reminded of this gift, spend a moment to silently give thanks for being the recipient. Notice how this changes your experience. Then, at the end of the day, spend some time reflecting on how your life would be different if you didn't have this element of your life permanently. Use the empathy you are cultivating to connect with others' daily experience. Spend a few moments sending all those you have connected with positive wishes. You can do this in writing, or just in your mind.

CHAPTER 8

Tools for Gratitude

TOOL 1: SELF-ASSESSMENT

There are several self-assessment tools online that could be used as a reflective measure for establishing baseline levels of gratitude. One of these is The Gratitude Questionnaire, or GQ-6. This is a six-question assessment, so it's easy to take and score. It doesn't, however, provide any specific information for how to respond to scores.

Another tool is Greater Good's Gratitude Quiz. This resource is 16 questions plus some demographic multiple-choice answers. I like this resource because it helps to reflect on the different ways one might be more grateful through the questions it asks: first in appreciating the positive and seeing the gifts given, and secondly, recognizing good fortune and how others are not as fortunate.

The quiz also gives suggestions and links to other resources for how to increase gratitude. I would particularly recommend the "Give it Up" practice, which I connect to the day of fasting my husband and I do each year around the holidays. Consciously abstaining from something that brings comfort and joy is another tool that fosters empathy for others who go without.

Whichever self-assessment tool you use (both can be found on the Book Resources page online), spend a few minutes reflecting on your scores. You may ask yourself the questions:

- How grateful do I consider myself to be right now?
- What are my gratitude strengths?
- What are my areas to grow?
- What goals might I set for myself based upon my baseline score(s)?

TOOL 2: SETTING AN INTENTION

Setting a daily intention to be more grateful is one of the most powerful tools I teach. When I talk with people who have taken training with me, they consistently say the intention to cultivate gratitude still has an impact on their life (and the lives of their children or loved ones).

PATH 2: GRATITUDE

When we practice gratitude, our reality and experience become more positive and welcoming. The impact is visceral and experiential. Cultivating this intention is simple, as it is a natural outcropping of mindfulness practice more generally. As you become more aware, you see more things to be grateful for.

Set an intention to notice moments of joy and pleasure in your daily life. These may be fleeting, micro-experiences that you might otherwise miss: the quiet expectation of dawn, the silky coolness from curling your toes into the sheets in the morning while waking, and the nutty, roasted scent of fresh coffee brewing. Simple pleasures, yes, but also the stuff from which life is made. Your intention might look something like this:

I will notice the daily pleasures of being alive and remember to be grateful.

Combine this intention with the Beautiful Moments practice as a reflective tool. As you get better at noticing goodness, both your positive moments and your gratitude for them will grow.

TOOL 3: CONNECTING WITH MENTORS

For the topic of gratitude, there is one specific mentor I would like to focus on. Brother David Steindl-Rast is a Benedictine monk known for his writing, teaching, interfaith leadership, and expertise in gratitude. I first encountered Steindl-Rast as the voice narrating the five-minute viral video "Gratitude HD—Moving Art." (This is, by the way, a video I show in my gratitude workshops; I highly recommend watching it.) From that point I dove deeply into his resources, including his organization A Network for Grateful Living. Here are a few of the things I discovered:

David Steindl-Rast on happiness. "Want to be Happy? Be Grateful" is Steindl-Rast's TEDTalk on how gratitude leads to happiness. One of the main points in his talk is the difference between scarcity thinking, or operating through fear, and what I would describe as abundance thinking, or operating through a sense of gratitude or having enough.

Gratefulness.org on practicing gratitude. This website, published by A Network for Grateful Living, provides a wealth of resources on gratitude. I would specifically recommend the practices, some of which I have used personally and written about on my blog. Here are a few I would recommend:

- **Light a Candle:** This practice is a wonderful example of an online tool enhancing our humanity. Click "begin," and you will be guided to take a moment to pause and reflect on your purpose before lighting and then dedicating a candle that will burn for 48 hours. There is also the opportunity to get a link and leave the candle burning in a window until it goes out. I love this practice that combines personal ritual with a larger community through technology. Seeing all of the other dedications on the site helped me to feel connected to the struggles and joys of all those who participated.

- **Stop. Look. Go:** This is an informal practice that happens in the comings and goings of daily life and takes only a few minutes and some reflection. Here are the three parts, as described on my own website:

  1. **Stop.** This alone is a quite valuable practice. We live in a culture that is all productivity, rush, and noise. Can we take a moment and be still? What benefits might we experience if we do? In Steindl-Rast's words, we need to create "stop signs" in our lives that create a pause, and be still. Take a moment and reflect: where might you create a stop sign in your own life? What cue will you use as a reminder?

2. **Look.** Be curious about your own experience in this moment. What do you see? Hear? Feel? For what can you experience a sense of gratitude? You don't need to manufacture anything, and if something quite difficult is happening, there is no reason to try and change it. Perhaps you just remember that you are alive. That you are breathing. That there is no moment exactly like this one.

3. **Go.** What seed for action is this moment offering you? Living is art that you create. How can you make it beautiful for yourself? For others? Ask these questions, and wait patiently for an answer. When you get one, do it, act on the insight that comes from your own intuition and reflection.

Path 3: Growth

GET COMFORTABLE WITH BEING
UNCOMFORTABLE*

*as quoted in my Jillian Michaels fitness yoga DVD "Yoga Inferno"

The default human state is happiness
and contentment. If I'm not happy and
content, something is probably
wrong with me.

There is no default human emotion or
ideal state. Uncomfortable
emotions are part of being human,
and they can be sources of meaning
and transformation.

CHAPTER 9

Introduction to Growth

Fall, 2014

I am sitting in my Grandma Rose's living room and settling in for the hours of discussion ahead. It's a Thursday, and I have just driven 45 minutes to Grandma's house instead of driving 35 minutes the opposite direction to be home with my two kids and husband. I have been doing this once a week, every week, for the last couple of months and coming on the weekends when I can, too.

My grandma is dying. I am here because I can't imagine my life without her. My marriage is also falling apart, and maybe I should be at home, but I need to be with her. She needs to be with me, too.

Sometimes I am unsure how long I can keep doing this, losing my grandma so slowly and so quickly at the same time. Fearing her loss every day, but not knowing how much longer I can sustain the lifestyle I have created, one that revolves around her death.

When I come to visit, we talk through her life. She relives the good moments, but we spend quite a bit of time on the darker ones, too. Maybe we do this because I am comfortable with darkness, because I live in darkness right now. She tells me what it was like to go through a divorce to be with a man who died six years later. She retells the story of the one time she got drunk in her life — on Christmas Eve, right after her first husband was gone. How she called her brother to come and get the kids until the next day.

"I had never been alone," she said, "not until that night."

She confides in me the ways she feels she wasn't always a good mother. How hard it was to understand her adopted daughter who had a rare disease called Prader-Willi Syndrome. She describes struggling to understand the obsessive eating and difficult-to-manage behaviors that were part of the illness, and how when her daughter was young, she left too much responsibility on one of her sons, my dad, to take care of her.

She tells me what it feels like to be dying, how some people just shine now. She tells me she likes to watch people quietly and hear their laughter unfold in the air.

She doesn't often talk about the pain, but I can see how her body is changing. How her skin has turned ashen, how her arms and legs are thin as wisps.

She tells me dying is lonely; people don't want to talk about death. They pretend it isn't happening. I am the only one willing to acknowledge that her time is so limited now, she says.

She tells me many things. Some I will never repeat to anyone. Some that were terrible, or sad, or disturbing. I carry these things in my heart when I go up to my room after midnight to sleep five hours before getting up to go to work the next morning. These things lie heavy in my soul.

When I wake up in the morning to have breakfast with her before leaving, she says to me, "You are a life raft. It's like I'm drowning. You save me."

We have each other in this, but I don't know for how long. Sometimes the world feels dark with fog, and I just can't see through.

Fall, 2014

My grandma died today. She passed in a room she had described in a morphine haze as "just this color," the color she would paint her ballroom where we would all dance together. The room was filled with people who loved her; she was never alone there.

When she passed, I sat beside her on the bed, one hand on her body, the other gripped in my mother's fist. Mom kept saying, "Tell her it's okay to let go," but I knew she already had. She was gone from her body, but I could still feel her there. It felt like light and warmth.

The whole world changed today. I can't describe exactly how, but I see there is a before and an after. The me before didn't see a way forward; I felt heavy and hollow. The me after feels full of warmth and light — her warmth, her light. I miss her already, but it also seems, in some way, that she is more present than ever before. This feeling won't last, but I will always remember it.

I am sitting on the patio by myself now. People are worried about me, and they keep passing through, asking how I am doing. I scared people with the sounds I made when she died. I have lost so much, but I have gained something, too. Something hard to articulate just yet.

I listen to the water trickle down, a gentle waterfall leading to her Buddha statue planted in the pond I splashed through as a child. I have flashes of being five again, playing in the water and sunlight. I remember sitting here, wrapped in a towel on her lap. Grandma said to me, "God is in that tree," like God was everywhere. Now she is everywhere, too.

PATH 3: GROWTH

Fall, 2014

It's late November, the same month of her passing. My family and I are on our annual trip to Southern Ohio to stay in a cabin with wide windows facing leafless trees and clear, cold sky.

I am sitting in an overstuffed lounge chair reading Alan Watts as the crackling wood in the potbelly stove spreads warmth throughout the room. The words on the page are poignant: "Please. Wake. Up."

I take a deep breath and look around, inhaling the moment. My mom is curled up in the chair across from me. The trees are still and silent in the windows behind her. When she sees me looking, she smiles, though my eyes are full of tears. My two sons are piled on the couch, youngest on top of oldest, as they watch cartoons. Sawyer whispers to Jory and points at the screen, asking a question. As he does this, Jory reaches up and touches his cheek gently before answering. These mundane sensations — sounds of idle chatter, smoky scent of burning logs, view of barren trees and rolling hills outside — create both gratitude and pain. I know that this is all there is, this moment. It makes me happier and sadder than I can bear. Loss has illuminated life.

Reflection

Being present for my Grandma Rose's death experience and grieving her loss at a time in my life that was personally challenging in many other ways was emotionally overwhelming. There were days when I wished for an escape by any means necessary. There were also times when I wondered whether the fog that surrounded my every moment, making it hard to breath and to see, was ever going to lift.

It was also a time of deep learning for me, however. Through death, literal and figurative, I also experienced a rebirth of sorts. By reliving Grandma's life with her, I gathered knowledge and wisdom that comes from the ending of a 76-year journey. Though I didn't know it at the time, our spirits were being stitched together through her stories and reflections, which now feel as rich as my own life experiences and bring a closeness to her that I treasure.

Her death gave new meaning to life. I saw how dying is part of the process of living, not separate from it. In those final moments, with my mother gripping my hand tightly, Grandma's leaving this world felt like a birth experience. The room breathed with her, and as she let go, something new also came into existence.

Her experience is not common. People often go to sterile environments and enter a stranger's care in the final moments (or even years) of their life. Perhaps this is one contributing factor to our death-averse culture. We no longer face the experience of dying as part of our ongoing lives. We don't have a chance to look it in the eyes before it's our turn.

In my grandma's case, not so. We were the ones fortunate enough to care for her. To wash her cringing body softly when she could no longer move. To hold vigil through the night and sweep her mouth clean when she could no longer swallow. These things may seem ugly on the surface, but within these acts, meaning is made.

This story of literal death relays a truth. We are all dying, every moment. There is the physical death that comes at the end of our lives, but also an emotional death that comes every time our circumstances change and we are asked to relinquish a part of ourselves.

When my grandma died, I felt clearly that nothing would be the same. My life was in a transition. Eventually, leaving my job became a part of this shift. I decided to go to a theological school in the area, and was not able to continue working in my position as an instructional coach at the same time. With a flailing marriage and no guaranteed financial security, my future safety was at stake in more ways than one with this decision, and I didn't even know exactly what I would be returning to school to do.

The transition was one of the hardest of my life. I

cried, frequently. The grief from losing Grandma and my own fears of the future swept me into a depressive episode that left me almost incapacitated. This reached a crescendo one day when I called off from work and instead spent the morning in bed crying. Almost instinctively, I grabbed the laptop beside me and typed in the search engine "symptoms of depression." I had every single one. That day I went to the doctor and was officially diagnosed: major depression and generalized anxiety.

There are many reasons I had fallen so deeply into emotional unrest, some of them chemical. At the same time, so much of my suffering was tied to my desire to avoid the unknown and resist the changes in my life. When everything that we identify as "us" is put into question, the impulse can be to cling to whatever we can grab to remain steady. A huge part of "me" was my role as a teacher and a friend to my colleagues. With this loss, and the insecurity of everything else that seemed to be slipping through my fingers, I was worried that I would disappear. The same was true with my diagnosis. The "me" who was strong enough to manage life on her own no longer existed. I grieved her loss and wasn't accepting of the diagnosis that seemed to stand in her place. This, too, is a kind of death — a death of the self.

I had yet to realize that even while life as I knew it was falling away, my personal truth was becoming more clear. We can learn to hide behind our own lives, identifying so much with our circumstances that we believe they are us. But as the Buddhist nun Pema Chödrön[3] says, "Only to the extent that we expose ourselves over and over to annihilation can that which is indestructible be found in us." Change can feel like annihilation, but when the fires have burned away all that is superfluous, the core of what's left is sometimes our gift, our truth, to carry into all that is after.

---

3 On a personal note, as the introduction stated, in the dark times of my life, I used the words of others to make meaning from my experiences. There are two teachers and texts who were particularly helpful at this time. One was Chödrön's book *When Things Fall Apart: Heart Advice for Difficult Times*. The other was the Franciscan monk Richard Rohr's book *Falling Upward: A Spirituality for the Two Halves of Life*.

CHAPTER 10

The Path Toward Growth

There is much research on the benefits of gratitude and mindfulness, and there is developing research on the benefits of some adversity as well. This path is about combining the proven benefits of awareness and acceptance from mindfulness practice and the benefits of reflection from a gratitude practice to the true nature of reality: adversity. When we can create meaning from dark experiences, we may find that this is where the richest of our life's fruits are rooted. This doesn't eliminate the pain, which is a necessary part of being human. It does, however, help to combat the urge to avoid and protect ourselves from parts of life we fear but will all face: grief, suffering, and loss.

PATH 3: GROWTH

Transformational adversity is humanity's oldest story. One could almost say it is *the* human story. It runs deep in every major religion and myth, and is the arc of the modern narrative:

1. Human is walking through life only somewhat satisfied.
2. Human encounters difficulty that shakes up his or her world.
3. Human learns something life-changing in the process of dealing with difficulty.
4. Human resolves, or doesn't resolve, the challenge and is gifted with a new understanding of the world, deeper relationships, or a more authentic expression of self.

Acceptance of our dark times is key, because suffering is embedded into this narrative arc. Modern culture, however, sometimes portrays happiness as the "default" human condition, concluding that difficult mental and emotional states are transitory distractions from happiness, and perhaps even atypical. Psychotherapist Tori Rodriguez describes this cultural shift, stating, "In recent years I have noticed an increase in the number of people who also feel guilty or ashamed about what they perceive to be negativity. Although positive emotions are worth cultivating, problems arise when people start believing they must be upbeat all the time." Our culture of perpetual happiness stifles authenticity because it's simply not true to the human experience. Furthermore, believing there is something "wrong" or "bad" about negative emotions limits vulnerability and facilitates repression and shame.

The old adage "the flies are part of the picnic" portrays a deep truth. Darkness and light occur on a continuum and need one another to accentuate their true nature. Each is integral to the human experience, and to truly dive into the depths of your own growth, you will feel both with equal intensity.

Adversity is one of the primary opportunities for human growth. Marriage and Family Therapist Linda Graham states, "The more difficulties you have, in fact, the greater opportunity there is to let them transform you. The difficult things…[become] the moment of truth." The field of psychology confirms that challenges can create transformational change that might not have occurred otherwise. This phenomenon is called post-traumatic growth, and it can include changes in the following categories:

1. **Opportunity:** A recognition of previously unseen possibilities and options
2. **Relationships:** A deepening and strengthening of one or more relationships; a growing sense of

empathy for all those in pain

3. **Strength:** A renewed sense of personal empowerment
4. **Gratitude:** A greater appreciation and awe for the experience of living
5. **Spiritual Growth/Depth:** A deepening sense of one's spiritual existence, possibly accompanied by shifting beliefs

Post-traumatic growth does not occur for everyone. There is, however, a key truth for many who have experienced it: the loss or challenge faced meant accepting the reality of never "coming back together" in the same way again. Something died, something was birthed, and never the twain shall meet.

Many who have faced adversity — the death of a loved one, the loss of a meaningful relationship, a major illness, or something else — understand that it is through this fire that the inessential is burned away and the most primary and necessary is exposed. In times of adversity, what is not working breaks down and fails, and what is most important is discovered. At the same time, if we continue to grasp for the past and what we had, then new learning never occurs. Instead, we are lost in longing for something that no longer exists.

Despite limitations to this truth, humans have the power of transformation even in — perhaps especially in — the times of most difficulty. This pivotal capacity is contingent upon the individual's ability to release the gravity of all that came before and fall into the weightlessness of the unknown. This is something to be extremely grateful for.

Knowing that something good may come out of a difficult experience will not stop pain and suffering. It is not an easy process to be present for the hardest times of life, and it may be tempting to repress or numb feelings. However, denial of emotions is the opposite of mindfulness, and can in fact lead to less growth. In times of distress, it is helpful — when possible and when the time is right for you — to connect with experiences and feelings the difficulty created in order to better know the needs that are arising. Awareness through mindfulness can facilitate this process.

I have had the same best friend since I was sixteen. She has seen me through many ups and downs, and warns me when she sees that I am feeling overwhelmed:

"Brandi, are you eating? You look really thin."
"Are you taking care of yourself? There is a lot going on right now."

I sometimes need these check-ins because I can disconnect from my own experiences in times of stress, becoming numb to emotions and even physical sensations.

I may not even notice that I'm hungry, for example.

For a long time, I didn't realize how much my stomach is a gauge for my mental health. I didn't connect my sometimes constant pain with stress. However, with the increased awareness developed through my practice, I can now better meet my own needs. If I begin to feel depressed or too anxious, my stomach is a gentle warning to take care of myself, and if ignored, it becomes an alarm. We all have things like this, but we need self-awareness in order to care for ourselves when these signals arise. When I start receiving these signs from my body, I now try to listen and act accordingly, spending more time outside and making sure to exercise and rest. I have learned these things help because I pay attention, which means caring for my own body in a way that I was incapable of doing before.

Once aware of difficult emotions, it is also important to reach out to others. According to Stanford Professor Kelly McGonigal's research on stress, challenges release oxytocin, which encourages connection and is considered a "feel good" hormone. If this craving is followed through with action, then stressful and challenging life circumstances can deepen connections to others as we seek to share experiences and find comfort. This is a proven way to increase resilience.

Conversely, when a person is suffering alone, the relational benefits of stress and challenge don't come to fruition. In addition, hidden distress does not disappear. In fact, hiding negative thought patterns and emotions can actually emphasize what you are trying to avoid. In a much-cited study led by Harvard Professor Daniel Wegner, one group of participants who were told to avoid thinking about white bears was compared to a control group who were not given these same instructions (as cited in Winerman 2011). Later, when the experiment group was told that the ban on white bears had been lifted, they actually thought about them more than the control group did. Expanding on this concept, consciously avoiding unwanted internal stimulus can bring even more attention to it later on. Instead, holding pain and discomfort in one's awareness compassionately and learning to share our distress with others are strategies that can contribute to the growth process that sometimes accompanies difficulty. These are skills that can be learned.

The first step is becoming conscious of our internal states. Recognizing the physical sensations that come with negative emotions and naming the emotions we are feeling can be helpful. When doing this, remember these experiences are fleeting and transitory. We can choose to act upon them or not. Mindfulness creates a space to both develop curiosity about our feelings and to create freedom to make choices rather than act from places of pain unconsciously.

Part of the human experience is built upon suffering;

you might say it is the price of growth. It is a price that can make life truly meaningful, however. With tools such as awareness, acceptance, and personal reflection, the chances of creating meaning and experiencing growth from pain are increased.

CHAPTER 11

Growth Practices

REFRAMING CHALLENGES

Time Commitment: 15 minutes

Frequency: Once in the next two weeks, and as desired afterward

Resources: Paper and pen or pencil

Optional Online Resource: Reframing Challenges Worksheet

We have all experienced difficulties in life. This practice is a way to reframe past challenges as opportunities for growth. In doing so, we create meaning and have the opportunity to live with a greater sense of purpose. We better understand how we have been resilient, and how we might move forward when other new challenges present themselves.

1. **Begin by taking a moment to reflect on some of the difficulties you have had to overcome.** These can be challenges you might consider small, but also any larger adversities you have experienced. On my own list, I included getting bullied as a child and teen, becoming a single mother at 18, not being offered teaching jobs I had hoped for, and being diagnosed with depression and anxiety, along with other life events already noted in this chapter and more not included. Please notice that this list includes my entire life. We begin building resilience at a young age.

2. **The following is one list of qualities[4] that you may have developed because of these experiences.** Take a few moments and read over this list, adding others you don't see that you think are important if needed.

---

4 Some of these qualities were taken from "The Personal Values Card Sort" by Miller, Baca, Mathews, and Wilbourne, a public-domain tool available online.

Perspective	Compassion	Hope
Wisdom	Generosity	Inner peace
Maturity	Self-knowledge	Knowledge
Gratitude	Love	Moderation
Resilience	Safety	Openness
Laughter	Creativity	Purpose
Strength	Family	Responsibility
Self-confidence	Flexibility	Realism
Acceptance	Genuineness	Tolerance
Achievement	Growth	Simplicity
Empathy	Honesty	

3. **Choose as many of the life challenges as you would like.** Use the following stem to reframe the experience as a tool you used to grow.

I experienced _____ *(challenge) and gained* _____ *(qualities).*

Here are some examples from my own list:

- I experienced bullying, and gained compassion, self-knowledge, and strength.
- I experienced becoming a single mother as a teenager, and gained maturity, family, and responsibility.

- I experienced not getting a job, and gained resilience and flexibility.
- I experienced being diagnosed with depression and anxiety, and gained honesty, realism, and acceptance.

4. **When you encounter a new challenge, come back to this list.** Inventory the skills and qualities you have developed that may help you cope, building self-confidence and facilitating a healthy framework of resilience.

FINDING GUIDANCE WITHIN

Time Commitment: 15–20 min.

Frequency: Once in the next two weeks, and as desired afterward

Resources: Paper; pen or pencil; a timer (for the version of this activity that uses an image); and a poem, short prose selection, or an image that speaks to you

Optional Online Resources: Links to poems and images

Whenever change and growth happens, there is a gap between leaving the old and finding the new. In this gap, confusion and ambiguity can result from having to make choices without all of the information we want. For many (myself included), this is sometimes quite difficult and stressful.

However, humans are meaning-making creatures. We have all experienced this capacity in our seemingly ceaseless extrapolation based on only the smallest bits of information: a look, a tone, a pause before a sentence — all of this is fodder for endless conjecture and storytelling. This capacity can be detrimental if the meaning we make from a stimulus does not serve us. We have all had the experience of mulling over a situation and interpreting it in ways that make us feel worse about ourselves and our circumstances.

However, we can also take advantage of our ability to make meaning. The world around us can be grist for the mill — fuel for deeper inquiry into what we feel and want. The Finding Guidance Within strategy is intended to facilitate just this process. In the same way that modern, secular mindfulness was inspired by the Buddhist tradition, this practice is a modern, secular version of Lectio Divina, a contemplative practice used in the Christian tradition to read and reflect on scripture.

Finding Guidance Within is my own version of this secularized practice. I use it personally and in my workshops as a fruitful way to harness our desire and ability to make meaning from all stimuli that we encounter. Like mindfulness, there is no faith requirement to use Finding Guidance Within (though if you practice a faith tradition, you can use this with any spiritual text you might feel inclined to explore). My version of the practice is about exploring our meaning-making faculties as tools for facilitating deeper reflection and enhanced inner guidance.

Finding Guidance Within, Text Version

The directions for using this practice with text are as follows.

1. **Choose a short text (poem or a section of prose) that is compelling for you.** It may evoke emotions, it may relate to something you are experiencing, or it may be intriguing to you for some other reason.

2. **Read the piece of text once just to listen.** It may help to read it out loud.

3. **Read the piece a second time, and notice what word, phrase, or sentence stands out to you the most.** You don't have to know why. If you would like, you can jot down this word, phrase, or sentence

before the next reading. (You can also write down any thoughts you may have for the remaining steps as well.)

4. **Read the piece a third time, continuing to focus on the words that stand out to you.** Ask yourself: "What am I hearing in this word or phrase right now? Is there some connection to my own experience that might be worth exploring?"

5. **Read the piece a fourth and final time, and ask yourself:** "What action, if any, do I want to take based upon what I am hearing?"

6. **If there is an action you want to take, commit to doing so.**

If you are seeking inspiration to try this practice, here are a few poets whose work I recommend: Rainer Marie Rilke, Nikki Giovanni, David Whyte, Mary Oliver, Rumi, Jimmy Santiago Baca, Kahlil Gibran, and Pablo Neruda. A collection of specific possibilities can be found on the On Being webpage, "The Poetry Radio Project." The radio show On Being by Krista Tippett often features poetry and poets, and on this page, you will find both full-text poems and recordings of poems read aloud. This is helpful if you prefer to listen to, rather than read, your poem of choice for the practice. (You will notice works from many of the poets I mentioned found here.)

Finding Guidance Within, Image Version

The directions for using this practice with images are as follows:

1. **Choose an image that is compelling for you.** This image should evoke emotion or intrigue.

2. **Spend a few minutes just looking at the image.** Look closely. Notice color, texture, and shape. Force your eyes to explore all parts of the image, maybe starting in one corner and roaming around each side before coming back to the center. It's key to bring as much of your focus to the image as possible.

3. **Grab a pencil and paper, and set a timer for five minutes.** When the timer begins, start writing, and try not to stop until the time is up. It doesn't matter what you write; just keep your pen or pencil moving on the paper. You may want to use the imagery you have studied as inspiration. You may explore a thought or memory that the image evokes for you. The main goal is to keep writing.

4. **When the timer goes off, go back and skim what you have just written.** Circle any words or phrases that stand out to you. It may be a phrase that is repeated. It may be a word that appeals to you, or even seems out of place. You should take only a minute to do this; don't think too much about it.

5. **After you have circled words, put them in a list.** Look at the list, and ask yourself the question: "What am I hearing in these words right now? Is there some connection to my own experience that might be worth exploring?" Answer the question in writing.

6. **After you have answered this question, ask yourself:** "What action, if any, do I want to take based upon what I am hearing?" Answer the question in writing.

7. **If there is an action you want to take, commit to doing so.**

In my workshops, I often choose images that are nature-based. This may be my bias, but I find nature is accessible to most everyone. You may also want to consider a piece of artwork, too. For example, the photographs of Robert and Shana ParkeHarrison are quite evocative and open to many interpretations. I have used

ParkeHarrisons' images to engage groups in a lively discussion of theme and meaning many times.

Notes

The key to this practice in either the visual or text-based form is to be reflective, honest, and open. More often than not, we know the answers to the questions in our lives if we listen hard enough. However, the input and perspective of others, and even society, can get in the way of what we really want and need. This process doesn't magically reveal anything that wasn't there before; it creates time, space, and openness to explore what already exists.

CULTIVATING FORGIVENESS

Time Commitment: 20 minutes

Frequency: Once in the next two weeks, and as desired afterward

Resources: Paper and pen or pencil

Optional Online Resources: Cultivating Forgiveness Worksheet

Often in times of difficulty, there are people we feel compelled to blame — both ourselves and others. This blame can lead to anger, resentment, and an inability to move forward. However, forgiveness can help to free us from these emotions. I have been on the giving and receiving end of forgiveness and have seen its powerful effects. I needed to receive my husband's forgiveness in order for our relationship to be mended. Conversely, there have been many times I have had to forgive others in order to continue relationships that were meaningful for me, even when it was painful to do so. Any time there is intimacy and love, there is also the ability to hurt one another. Connection creates a strong likelihood that we will both need to give and receive forgiveness at many points in our lives from many people.

I was recently in the process of forgiving a close friend for what felt to me like deep betrayal. The initial event happened over a year ago, and months after finding out about it, I was still processing. As part of my reflection, I posted a request on Facebook to hear what others have done to facilitate forgiveness. My post reflected on a sentiment, a short poem called "How to Forgive" by Hana Malik. With her permission, the poem is as follows,

Forgiveness is
Taking the knife out your own back
and not using it

to hurt anyone else
no matter how
they hurt you.

I loved these words, because to me, they made clear the personal responsibility we have in our own pain. Resentment, anger, shame, and sorrow may be a natural reaction to a hurtful circumstance. At the same time, if we don't take personal responsibility for both healing and becoming aware of how our injuries may affect the ways we act toward others, then we are at fault. This is the idea that began my own forgiveness journey. It felt empowering.

In responses to my post, some people expressed long (and sometimes arduous) journeys toward forgiveness in their own lives. In addition, one woman made a suggestion to write a letter of forgiveness to the person who had caused pain. While it took me a few weeks to be ready, this was something I eventually did. Writing and sending the letter helped to free me from some of the emotional residue that the situation had created. It felt good.

To be realistic, however, writing this letter was only one stage of my forgiveness. When the person responded (and I now wish I had asked them not to), I once again got caught up in feeling offended by their reactions. In addition, I still had negative feelings about the person and the original situation. Going back to the collective wisdom of my friends, this connects with something someone else said in response to my post, which is that forgiveness is a daily practice, rather than a single event. That even as we forgive, the pain still lingers and may have to be addressed again and again. This, too, is true in my experience.

Forgiveness is circuitous. There is no one in this world who cannot use it, and there is no one in this world who cannot give it. We have all caused and received pain. That's the messiness of being human.

Case in point, when I posted the short poem about forgiveness and asked for input, someone responded unexpectedly. I had done something to hurt this person tremendously and had never had the chance to say I was sorry, as we had not been in contact for a long time. The post started a private message conversation where I apologized and experienced forgiveness. It was this person's ability and desire to engage that ultimately led to my own quest toward forgiveness of another through writing a letter.

There is no magic formula for easy forgiveness, because situations where it is most needed may evoke pain, sadness, anger, and shame. We might desire consciously or unconsciously to repress or ignore these feelings. We might do the opposite and feel the urge to simmer in them. It can be a long process. Feeling hurt and reacting in all kinds of ways is natural; everyone heals differently. Just knowing that forgiveness is a type of self-healing may help. When we forgive others and forgive ourselves, we are tenderly dressing a wound, protecting ourselves from later damage and minimizing the extent of our injury.

Think about how you might integrate forgiveness into your own life. Are there things for which you can forgive yourself? Forgive others? The following steps may help you to identify these areas:

1. **Make two lists, side by side.** In the first list, write down the ways you have been hurt by others and are still healing. This first list is a tool for you to reflect on how you might cultivate forgiveness for others. To begin, choose one specific item on the list. Maybe start with a transgression that is less painful for you. Ask yourself to imagine what hurt, insecurity, or fear that person may have had that motivated the person to behave in ways that caused you pain. See whether you can understand the person's intentions, motivations, or feelings to even the smallest degree. If possible, wish for peace for the person who hurt you. This is one practice you can use while working with this list.

2. **In the second list, write down ways you have caused someone else to hurt.** This second list is a tool to both make amends where necessary and

also cultivate self-forgiveness. Choose one item from the list, and hone in on it. First, consider whether there is some action you could take that would help make amends to this person. Once you have addressed this question, then consider whether you can begin to forgive yourself for this transgression. Using the same empathy practice you used in the first list, ask yourself whether you can see what hurt, insecurity, or fear may have contributed to the action that caused this person pain. Try wishing for both your own peace of mind and peace of mind for the person you hurt.

3. **Finally, look at these two lists side by side.** Are there ways that you have hurt others that might help you to empathize with those who have hurt you? Conversely, can you recognize that others have caused pain, too, and that you are not alone in having made mistakes? See if you can use these two lists to develop a sense of the common humanity you share with all people, both those who have hurt others and those who are hurting.

This practice is only one possible step toward greater forgiveness. Our lists may change and shift over time. Forgiveness is a daily journey of being gentle with ourselves and others, recognizing that we each make mistakes and that we all deserve compassion and empathy.

CHAPTER 12

Tools for Growth

TOOL 1: SELF-ASSESSMENT

One self-reflective tool for assessing how past challenges have contributed to positive outcomes is the Post Traumatic Growth Inventory (PTGI), which can be found on the book resources page online. The assessment does not give ranking categories, such as high or low growth. It is instead helpful in thinking about the areas in which you have grown. The scale lists five areas: 1. Relating to Others, 2. New Possibilities, 3. Personal Strength, 4. Spiritual Change, and 5. Appreciation of Life. There are questions relating to each of these on the scale.

Another way of using these growth categories to

facilitate self-reflection might be to choose a difficult life event, and then consider in writing how it changed each of these five areas of your life. I've listed below some example questions you might consider. Keeping the event and any changes you experienced because of it in mind, answer any or all of the prompts that apply.

- Which of your relationships grew stronger, or did any new relationships develop?
- How has your empathy deepened?
- What new opportunities were you offered?
- What personal strengths did you recognize or develop?
- How do you now see yourself differently in ways that are helpful because of this experience?
- How do you now see the world differently in ways that are helpful because of this experience?
- What shifts in belief or mindset were beneficial to you because of this experience?
- How did the event strengthen your spiritual life?
- How has your sense of gratitude, wonder, and awe been further developed?

As you explore these questions, you are developing a new narrative for your life. These stories are powerful resources. Telling them to ourselves and to others facilitates meaning-making and highlights personal strength.

PATH 3: GROWTH

In a communications workshop I co-facilitated for men living with HIV and AIDS, we practiced reflecting on and sharing stories of resilience. Many of the men decided to explain how their diagnosis had changed their lives for the better. A common turning point in the stories was learning to be open about their disease with others, even though they were afraid of being stigmatized. Taking control of their own narrative was part of the healing process, as it is for so many of us. Listening to these men affirmed for me that sharing through the lens of resilience affects our own self-acceptance and even our perceptions of reality.

TOOL 2: SETTING AN INTENTION

Intentions use the power of awareness and attention to harness our ability as humans to grow from challenges. Set a personal intention to frame difficult experiences as growth opportunities. In order to focus your growth on an area that is most beneficial, choose one of the five growth categories in which you would like to grow, and write out an intention related to that category. As a reminder, these are:

1. Relating to Others
2. New Possibilities
3. Personal Strength
4. Spiritual Change

5. Appreciation of Life

For example, let's say that I am interested in improving my ability to relate to others. My intention might be something like:

I will use difficulties I encounter today as opportunities to strengthen my ability to build healthy relationships.

This intention statement can also be used as a stem for other goals:

I will use difficulties I encounter today as

_____.

Throughout the day, you might remind yourself of this intention when difficulties arise, perhaps asking:

How can I use _____ as an opportunity to strengthen my ability to build healthy relationships?

At the end of each day, make it a practice to be self-reflective through journaling, asking yourself the following questions:

- What difficulties did I face today? How did I use them as opportunities for growth?

- How would I handle this situation in a way that is most aligned with my intention if I were to encounter it again?
- What successes did I have?
- How can I build on these successes in future similar situations I may encounter?

TOOL 3: CONNECTING WITH MENTORS

There are so many wonderful resources that help to encourage growth from difficulty and increase resilience in the face of challenges. The field of education, for example, is rife with research on grit, growth, resilience, and the power of mindset. Here are some of the researchers and writers I most respect. For each, I will mention a few key resources and summarize a bit of their work.

Carol Dweck on growth mindset. Dweck has a TED-Talk called "The Power of Believing You Can Improve" and a book called *Mindset: The Psychology of Success.* Her name is synonymous with growth mindset, which is basically the belief that our traits — such as intelligence — are not fixed. One simple way to develop growth mindset is to expose people to the science, which is what Dweck recommends. In her TEDTalk, Dweck explained that part of her research is to tell students that, "every time they push out of their comfort zone to learn something new and difficult, the neurons in their brain can form new, stronger connections, and over time they can get smarter." This process of brain change continues throughout life, as long as we are willing to try new things and embrace challenges.

Angela Lee Duckworth on grit. Duckworth has a TEDTalk called "Grit: The power of passion and perseverance" and a book by the same name. As part of her research, she created a grit scale that can be found online. This may be a helpful tool for self-assessment. She has made major strides in understanding motivation, which she describes as grit. In her TEDTalk, she explains that grit is "passion and perseverance for very long-term goals. Grit is having stamina. Grit is sticking with your future, day in, day out, not just for the week, not just for the month, but for years, and working really hard to make that future a reality. Grit is living life like it's a marathon, not a sprint." Dweck also explains in her TEDTalk how growth mindset is one tool for teaching and growing grit.

Linda Graham on resilience. Graham is a Marriage and Family Therapist who wrote a book on resilience called *Bouncing Back: Rewiring Your Brain for Maximum Resilience.* In her book, she describes how neuroplasticity allows us to change our brains to be more resilient. She relies heavily on research, but also converts that research into practical activities and skills that readers can use to take advantage of the insights. My copy of this book is well-worn, and the insights infuse my work with others.

Kelly McGonigal on stress. McGonigal has a TEDTalk called "How To Make Stress Your Friend" and a book called *The Upside of Stress: Why Stress is Good for You, and How to Get Good At It*. In her research, she explains how the belief that stress is bad for us is what creates all of the negative mental and physical health factors associated with it (unbelievable but true). She also describes the positive benefits of some types of stress and the protective factors in times of duress. My favorite of these is referenced in this chapter: connection is both a protective factor and an effect of stressful circumstances. Her book gave me a whole new perspective on how important meaning, purpose, and relationships are to our physiology and mental and physical health.

MYTHS OF BEING HUMAN

Path 4:
Connection

EMBRACE YOUR DEPENDENCE

myth #4

Humans are independent individuals whose main concern is personal success and achievement.

---

reality #4

Humans are a social species, and we are wired for compassion and interconnection.

CHAPTER 13

Introduction to Connection

Fall, 2012

I am meeting a friend after work. It has become our ritual to go to a local pizza shop for happy hour. It's hard for me to build deep connections with people, and so I am grateful to have this friendship.

There are parts of myself I have forgotten as an adult. The part that loved the way words flowed from my subconscious onto the blank page when I was writing. The part that thought there was some secret to the universe that I was always on the cusp of discovering, even in the most mundane daily experiences. The part that sat for hours parsing language, finding the world in a word. There is another part now, too — a more recent, secret part that is sad and wondering what else there is to life. Somehow I see those parts, even lay claim to them, when I am with him. It's nice, rare even, to feel understood.

We're on our second pitcher when I look at the clock. It's 8:00 p.m. We have been here for hours. This happens more often then I would like to admit, and we joke about it on Monday. "Did you get in trouble?" I ask.

"No. How about you?"

"Me neither."

Fall, 2013

It's a Saturday morning, and the kids are staying with my parents, so Jamey and I are alone. I have followed him into the bathroom while he is getting ready, and I am frantically trying to explain something to him, hands waving while I talk.

"Listen to me. We are not okay," I say, practically yelling, "…. I have feelings for someone else."

He looks at me seriously, and I feel a shift has occurred between the two of us. The wall isn't gone, but the foundation is unsteady.

I say the words again, "We…are…not…okay."

"Okay," he says. "We'll start counseling."

I breathe a sigh of relief.

CONNECTION

Winter, 2014

I have been sitting in the snow-covered backyard wrapped in a comforter, chain-smoking cigarettes while fighting off the icy cold.

My brain feels on the verge of collapse. I am going to tell Jamey it's over. I can't do this anymore. The counseling hasn't helped, and my feelings aren't changing. This is just too hard. My body feels like it's being ripped in half.

Jamey is home early, a strange occurrence. He finds me huddled in the yard. "We need to talk," I say to him.

"I know," he says. "I'm worried."

After we pick up the kids, we ask our oldest to babysit while we go on a "date." At dinner, we are both crying. Jamey finally tells me, for the first time, what he is seeing.

"You are just not present. Not with me. Not with the kids. You should talk to them about it and see what they say. It makes me really sad." Eyes full of tears, he continues, "I used to blame you, but I don't anymore."

He tells me this and more. How hurt he feels when I don't call, or when I tell him I'll be home at a certain time and don't make it. How destructive it can be to the kids when I am wrapped up in my own world for hours and don't hear their voices calling for my attention and love. He tells me he feels like he has taken on too much in our household, because I am just not there, sometimes physically, but many times emotionally.

He is lonely, too.

Spring, 2014

It's almost time to go and pick up the kids after school. I leave the house for the short walk to Sawyer's elementary building and try to clear my mind of the residue from the day with a few deep, cleansing breaths.

When I walk in the door of his after-school classroom, Sawyer smiles widely and jumps into my arms as I lean down to greet him. I soak up the warmth of his little body and press my cheek to his in a dramatic embrace before we leave.

We hold hands as we walk home, and he breaks away, yelling back to me, "Mommy, let's be horses! I want to race!" Thrusting his little body into a gallop, he whinnies down the sidewalk away from me. I follow, skipping and neighing alongside him for the two blocks back to the house. When we arrive out of breath, I clear my cell phone and laptop from the dining room table and put them into my bag. I won't look at them again tonight. Sawyer and I go into the kitchen together, and I get out the cutting board and chef's knife.

This is our ritual. He sits on the counter as I chop vegetables, grabbing and tasting chunks of raw celery, carrot, and even potato (which he will later refuse to eat in the soup). I listen to the soothing sound of blade on wood and engage in childish banter, leaving behind any events from the rest of my day.

"Hello, family!" I hear Jamey yell from the front door as he and Jory enter.

"Daddy! Jory!" Sawyer yells back, as I lower him from the counter and take the opportunity to squish a kiss onto his cheek.

Later, the four of us will sit down to dinner together, as we do every night. We will follow our routine of sharing a fulfilling thing and a challenging thing from our day before we clear the table and clean the kitchen together.

We will spend the early evening in the yard playing a nonsensical game of football where Sawyer always wins and Jory inevitably lifts him up to the sky in a way that is simultaneously joyful and terrifying.

We will all curl up in bed together as Sawyer reads his book to us. After he is settled for sleep and Jory goes to study in his room, I will have my nightly quiet time where I practice mindfulness and journal alone.

Later, when the kids are in their rooms, and Jamey and I are alone, he will have bourbon and I will have tea. We will not turn on the television. We will instead sit in the too-small-for-two window seat or lay side-by-side in bed reviewing our day, sharing the things we are reading, reminiscing about something the kids did.

Tomorrow I will get up and do this all again.

Reflection

Along my journey of growth, recognizing my unrealized need for connection and then having the insight that I was the one preventing it was one of the most transformative catalysts for change in my life. There were times when my emotions were too big for me to see around. I could focus only on my own needs with little to no recognition of how hurtful that was to those I loved. This damaged my relationship with my husband and my children. My emotions sometimes took up all of my oxygen, leaving little energy and life for growth or change, care and compromise.

It was truly so uncomfortable to not have my needs met that my actions ran on automatic. I acted out in anger, retaliated through dismissiveness, and tried anything to not feel the discomfort. Once I realized the damage I'd done, I still didn't know how to fix it. I only knew that it hurt to be disconnected, and it needed to be repaired. Having a partner (my husband) who showed me to myself clearly, the good and the bad, was a necessary catalyst for change, as painful as the circumstances may have been for both of us.

Before this catalyst, I was incapacitated. My "story" was that I was broken and misunderstood. That I was an ambitious creative who needed to follow her passions and a "free spirit" who needed to live her own, uninhibited life. Most deeply, though I would never admit it, there also lurked a belief that I was a little bit special and my needs were a little more important than those of others.

Of course, all of these beliefs about myself — I'm special, I'm different, I'm broken — all served to further alienate me from those I cared about, and even those I had just met. On countless occasions, I looked around a room and thought, "I don't belong here." How did I cope with this? I drank a bit too much, talked a great deal, and left most interactions without any real connection. I acted like an extrovert, but my banter was a shield protecting the stuff inside, the broken stuff.

Within me (and I think within all of us), the desire to be understood, to feel seen, runs deeply. When not addressed, this desire finds ways to get attention, and some of those ways can be counterproductive and damaging. Through my own yearning to fulfill this need, I invested much of my energy in a few close friendships. When one of those friendships became an emotional affair, removing myself from the situation felt overwhelming, verging on impossible.

I wasn't building healthy outlets for connection because I couldn't see myself or my relationships clearly. When my husband shared with me how my detachment was a barrier to meeting both my needs and my family's, he helped me get out of my own way. I needed him to tell me that he had felt hurt, confused, and disappointed in how I hadn't recognized what my family needed from me.

This is the part of connection that gets ugly. We all have a "story," a way we see ourselves that isn't true to reality. Because we see our own intentions and extenuating circumstances, we give ourselves leeway for our inappropriate behaviors:

Well, I was tired...
I had a right to do that because...
I was just trying to...so it's not my fault if...

At the same time, we don't see the intentions of others, so we don't give them that same privilege. Sometimes we need another person to be a mirror that reflects back our true selves. In that space, we will see the beauty we hide from ourselves, but perhaps even more importantly, we will see the many ways we have hurt others or avoided reality. Being able to do this in partnership with another person is true intimacy.

There is a quote from author James Hannaham's novel *Delicious Foods* that I use often in my work with others. Sirius, a character who provides the philosophical waxing for the story's themes, states, "... most often people who have power turn their story into a brick wall keeping out somebody else's truth..." I don't think it's just those in power who do this, however, though power can most certainly be a corrupting force. I think we all do this.

CONNECTION

Others' truths are painful. We unconsciously want to protect ourselves from them, especially if they involve us.

The changes I made in my life to reconnect with those closest to me and grow my compassion were not abstract; they were the daily work of living with others. Things such as putting what seemed important to *me* in a proper place among others' equally important needs. My creative work and my ability to be a free spirit are important, but *this* is important as well. Sometimes *this* is remembering to make an appointment for Jory, trying to have fun at a history museum because Jamey loves it, or doing homework with Sawyer (even when it's math). *This* is the stuff of love and connection.

As my grandma lived her final days with us, she spent her time mourning the loss of those she loved dearly and lamenting the moments she wasn't present for those she cherished. She also reveled in the connections and relationships she had been fortunate enough to keep (of which there were many). In the end, our biggest regrets and our biggest successes will all come from the ways we were disconnected from or connected to others. This is the stuff life is made of. I know this now. In the end, it all comes down to love.

Love is not glamourous. At times, in fact, it feels like a sickening careen into the abyss. More often than not, however, love is simply the dying embers of a smoky fire. It's the dried blades of grass and broken twigs we blow on, slowly and gently, hands cupped against the wind.

CHAPTER 14

The Path Toward Connection

There is a longing for deep connection within each of us. We can repress, deny, numb, or ignore this longing, but if it isn't met, it will leave a deep, aching need that can be filled no other way. This may sound like philosophy, possibly even sentimentality, but it is in fact science. The human brain is designed to be in meaningful contact with others. The path of connection and compassion brings the conscious attention of mindfulness to the ways humans are dependent on one another emotionally and physically on a deeper level than our articulated feelings or our conscious thoughts. Ignoring these connections can unknowingly cause damage to ourselves and others. Our implicit bonds with *everyone* in our environment are necessary for survival, and they are also the source of many of the greatest human joys.

Modern society is counterculture to the path of connection and compassion, however. American culture implies that success, popularity, and financial gain bring happiness, and this implication impacts our worldview. *The High Price of Materialism* author Tim Kasser and a team of researchers describe the effects of "materialistic value orientation" (MVO), which is a belief system which finds value in financial success, high status, and cultivating an image. People who operate from MVO have lower life satisfaction and are more likely to experience depression. They have lower self-esteem, less empathy, and are more focused on external rewards than internal satisfaction. Despite the fact that this value orientation doesn't serve humanity, it is deified in the media as the latest iteration of the American Dream. We live in a culture of consumerism. The higher the quality of the products we consume, the more successful our lives are perceived to be. The higher our status and the more public our image, the more we are admired. This ideology not only fails to create happiness, it actively prevents it.

Despite the individualistic and materialistic nature of modern industrialized culture, humans are most satisfied when they can give of themselves to others. According to Professor Elizabeth Dunn's research, individuals who reported higher levels of charitable giving reported more happiness than those who reported more self-related spending. This also includes windfall money. When individuals were given an envelope of cash to donate to charity, they self-reported more happiness than those who were given the same amount of cash to spend on themselves. This happiness has a neurological basis; charitable giving activates the reward center of the brain. This is true even when the giving remains anonymous. These findings are just inklings of the deeper reality of human evolution, which is not survival of the fittest, but instead a continuous adaptation of our complex and interwoven relationship systems.

The truth is our psychology and biology respond more positively to actions based on interconnectedness, not individualism. Connecting with others and showing compassion leads to physical and mental health benefits such as faster recovery from diseases, lower blood pressure, less depression and anxiety, a stronger immune system, a longer lifespan, and higher self-esteem. Conversely, individuals with the fewest social connections have been shown to be twice as likely to die earlier than those who maintain more robust connections.

Compassion and connection both have many benefits, and not just in personal life. Work settings with a culture of affectionate warmth and interconnection are correlated with a range of positive outcomes. Confirmed by a study conducted by professors of management Sigal Barsade and Olivia O'Neill, a culture of "companionate love" is highly correlated with higher work satisfaction, more teamwork, less burnout, and more personal accountability for employees. It is also correlated with higher client satisfaction.

The link between connected, caring relationships and the positive emotions and higher performance they elicit in the workplace is not random. It may be based on our evolutionary history. Some scientists believe that our interconnectedness is the single quality that defines humanity and enables our success as a species. Matthew Lieberman, researcher and author of the book *Social*, states, "To the extent that we can characterize evolution as designing the modern brain, this is what our brains were wired for: reaching out and connecting with others" (as cited in Cook, 2013). We are made for this.

Interconnectedness is deeply interwoven into the networks of the human brain, and the ways we are connected to others is a primary concern of the self. In a study by neuroscience researchers Kyle Simmons and Alex Martin, they found that the social-cognitive and default mode networks (DMN) of the brain overlap in areas. This means that the brain's resting state, or the state it defaults to when not engaged in a specific task, in part resides in areas associated with what they describe as "self-relevant (social), affective decisions." In other words, when we are not actively occupied with something else, there is a good chance we are thinking about how we are emotionally and socially connected or disconnected with others.

There is a building understanding that this hardwiring is perhaps exactly what has allowed humans to succeed despite our many physical defects compared to other species. When Jamil Zaki, Lab Director of the Stanford Social Neuroscience Laboratory, and Kevin Ochsner, Director of The Social Cognitive and Affective Neuroscience (SCAN) Lab at Columbia, collaborated to review on the neuroscience of empathy, they began by stating as much. They said, "Although many answers may be offered...psychologists increasingly believe that it is our interpersonal faculties, especially our ability to cooperate with and understand others, that have supported our species' success." The human abilities to maintain co-dependent relationships and to empathize with one another may be the facets of our neurobiology that have allowed us to maintain the ever-dominating role we play in our natural environment.

Similar to mounds collectively designed by ants or hives created by hundreds of bees, the sum of human interaction is greater than its parts. Through working toward common goals, intuiting others' emotions, communicating our needs, and hearing others' perspectives, something new and more substantial is created.

So what happens when individuals do not have access to the inherent interconnectedness that is our birthright? A lack of strong social connection has been linked to adverse health consequences, even more so than smoking or obesity. Professor Brené Brown is a researcher of the "whole-hearted," which is a state of being founded in a sense of worthiness. This worthiness expresses itself through the courage to be seen by others as our imperfect selves, and it leads to deeper, more connected relationships. Conversely, she is also a researcher of shame, which expresses itself as unworthiness and leads to disconnection in relationships. Shame is one cause of our disconnection from others, and it can lead to numbing through addiction, obsessive perfectionism, and indignant self-righteousness — all in an effort to avoid showing the damaged self we belief is unworthy of love, to avoid being vulnerable.

Brown further explains in an interview with author of *The Happiness Track*, Emma Seppälä, "We are biologically, cognitively, physically, and spiritually wired to love, to be loved and to belong. When those needs are not met, we don't function as we're meant to. We break apart. We fall apart. We numb. We ache. We hurt others. We get sick." What may on the surface appear to be existential angst, a feeling of disconnection or loneliness, is actually a profound and deeply rooted biological longing to connect to our own humanity through deep relationship. If the symptoms are not treated, the end result is continued and more extensive damage.

The cost of disconnection from others can be

measured in health risks and emotional pain, but most importantly, the cost may be losing who we really are. When connection isn't present, something seems "missing." That sense of loss can be pervasive, even as the cause remains elusive. A person might spend his or her whole life seeking fulfillment measured in square footage or bought with a credit card. Some might get lost in success and prestige, becoming those who survive life instead of living it. Others may hide within the guise of sarcasm or sleep through life under the influence of alcohol, drugs, food, or other addictions. We do all of this work to cover the emptiness and curb the appetite for something more. We want to avoid at all costs being deeply seen and felt by others as our flawed, imperfect selves. It's a life overflowing with doing and busyness, but empty of being and truth.

This type of life is not inescapable. Connecting with others and having compassion is a core part of who we are as humans. At the same time, connection and compassion are also skills and mindsets that can always be further developed and honed. Just because we are not connecting in this moment doesn't mean it's impossible. Just because we have fallen away from active compassion does not mean we are not compassionate. Perhaps we have only become distracted from this part of ourselves by the myriad of societal rewards that come with a self-focused worldview. The practices in the next chapter will provide tools for refreshing and enriching your own inherent sense of connection and compassion, helping you to move along the path of a more meaningful and human life.

CHAPTER 15

Connection Practices

MINDFUL LISTENING

Time Commitment: Varies

Frequency: Once in the next two weeks, and as desired afterward

Resources: None

Listening is a gift we choose to give to another human being; it helps the other person to feel "heard" or "seen." While hard to articulate, this intangible quality is often equated with feeling less alone. While we all know what it's like to have this experience, we may also be able to think of many other occasions when we felt as though we were not listened to or understood. This creates alienation and frustration.

There are so many distractions from being present that make it challenging to listen well, even when we want to. Because it is difficult, providing the gift of full presence for another can have a profound impact. We all crave this sense of another person "getting" what we are going through, but few of us receive it every time we want it.

Fortunately, listening is a skill that can be developed over time with purposeful practice; it is in no way magical or elusive. The development of mindful listening is a practice of full presence without being self-referential or having a personal agenda for the conversation. This is a difficult task aided by plenty of honest self-reflection and a genuine desire to grow.

The process begins by preparing our bodies to listen, which can send a powerful message of intention to ourselves and others. Our posture can be a visual cue that we are fully invested in a conversation. In my year as a counseling student, I learned that I had no idea what listening looks like. As an extreme example, throughout much of my professional life I sat in group meetings, shoes off, hugging my knees to my chest with my feet on the seat of the chair; this is far from appropriate listening posture. My body language told people that I was in protective mode, closed off from connection. (Not to mention it is perhaps not the most professional of postures.)

Since that time, I have developed the habit of open body language, a posture Dr. Fulgence Nyengele, professor at Methodist Theological School of Ohio, taught me when I was a counseling student. This posture is hard for me. It literally *feels* exposing, but I do it anyway because my goal in many conversations is to be vulnerable. The following is what listening looks like to me now. You can use this list as a general guideline or checklist when in conversations where you want to make sure the other person is feeling heard and supported by you.

1. **Point your body toward the person you are speaking to.** If possible, remove obstacles between the two of you, such as tables, laptops, cell phones, etc.

2. **Sit fully (but comfortably) upright.** Uncross your arms and legs so that you are sitting feet to the floor, hands on knees or thighs.

3. **Lean (slightly) toward the other person.**

4. **If culturally appropriate, maintain what is called "soft eye contact."** This is eye contact that is directed toward the center of the other person's face. It is a comfortable, relaxed way to maintain focus without seeming overbearing.

In addition to preparing our bodies to listen, we can also prepare our minds. I call this *listening inwardly*. Inward listening is maintaining a dispassionate awareness of the thoughts, sensations, and feelings present within one's self during a conversation. Sometimes we are thinking or feeling things that are barriers to our ability to listen, and with self-reflection, these circumstances can be addressed. For example, if I am really frustrated by something that just happened, I am probably going to be less compassionate about someone else's problems. I should take a few minutes and a few deep breaths by myself before having a meaningful conversation where I need to be a thoughtful listener.

Inward listening reflects and builds on the practice of mindfulness generally. The voice within can often be a barrier to the present moment if we invest too much in it, and it is also a distraction from hearing the words of another. For example, if I am in a conversation, the primary concern of the voice in my head might be how I appear to the other person.

Am I making a good impression?
Did I really just say that? She probably thinks I am an idiot.
If I say _____, I will sound clever, witty, intelligent, (etc.)

The list goes on. The voice in our heads is often preoccupied with creating, maintaining, and protecting a vision of who we are that is consistent and positive. This isn't necessarily bad, but when conversation becomes a vehicle to reinforce our self-image, we are doing little to benefit our connection with others.

Mindful listening does not attempt to make this voice stop, which may only create further distraction. It is instead about gaining right-sized perspective in order to ask the question, "What does this moment require of me right now?" More often than not, simply listening may be the answer. Good listening doesn't happen all at once. There are steps you can take to facilitate the process more consistently, however:

1. **Become aware of what's happening inside.** Take a moment to notice the thoughts, feelings, and sensations that are rippling through you. To practice this skill, close your eyes and ask, "What am I experiencing?" You may become aware of thoughts first, but then gently move your awareness to more subtle experiences. Do you notice any sensations? Any feelings? Can you bring awareness to your heartbeat? Your breathing? What else is present in your body? Become aware of how quickly experiences change, how transient and fleeting they are. As you quickly scan through your thoughts, feelings, and sensations, is there some prominent feature that needs your attention before you can listen? If so, see whether

you can take a moment to either take care of, or let go of, this feature.

2. **Practice dispassionate awareness.** Try watching your rippling thoughts, feelings and sensations without investing energy in them. Can you gain some distance from them, and become an observer instead of a participant? For example, can you believe that the voice inside of you is sometimes unreasonable? Can you decide not to believe an unhealthy story? Can you recognize that an uncomfortable emotion or sensation will pass with time, and that you have the stamina to sit with it instead of avoiding it? Try to approach your experiences with curiosity, not judgment.

3. **Do an outer stimulus scan.** What's happening in your environment? What do you notice? How is it affecting you and/or changing your inner experience? Ask yourself, "What is called for right now, in this moment?" If the answer is listening, then proceed to #4.

4. **Listen.** There will always be distractions and urges to pull away from this moment, but you can continue to gently bring your attention back to the interaction. This includes processing what the other person is saying and noticing all of the ways you react. Be

curious about this process as it unfolds. How do you know when you are listening? What are the cues? How does it feel to listen? What indicators can you gather about the other person's reactions to this process and emotional states?

Listening to someone else is just an extension of inner listening, and we are always doing both at the same time. In addition, even with some emotional distance from our own experiences, there will still be impulses for you to direct during a discussion. For example, you may have an impulse to think about what to share next:

"I know exactly what you mean! This one time I…" (followed by a 10-minute story)

While this may seem like a way to build connection, it also inserts the self back into focus and avoids the other person's truth. The person receiving the listening may even become preoccupied with your situation, shifting the conversational direction entirely. Sharing our stories is an important mechanism for identity-building and common humanity, but keep in mind your goal for the interaction. If it is to help another person feel heard and understood, then just being present may be the best strategy. If you feel like a personal experience is helpful to share, a few sentences can go a long way. "I remember when I experienced something similar. It was incredibly hard," for example.

There are many myths about listening disguised as common knowledge. Connecting with others through continual or verbose personal anecdotes is one of them. Here are a few others, along with suggestions for what to do instead:

1. **Asking questions is a good listening skill.** While questions need to be asked at times to gain clarity, once someone starts telling their story, they can become an impediment. A question can be a way for the listener to guide the conversation in a direction of his or her own interest, which can distract the speaker from the focal point of sharing. Questions can also be an attempt on the part of the listener to solve a problem for the person speaking, which is disempowering. For example, "Did you try...?" implies a solution-focused lens as opposed to a companionate lens.

    Instead, the listener can use the technique of mirroring. This is a process of repeating back what the listener is hearing:

    "So what I think I hear you saying is..."
    "You are feeling..."
    "This situation is..."

The tone of these statements should not be in the form of questions, but as Professor Nyengele so aptly modeled, your voice should actually become lower and deeper at the end of reflective statements. This has the affective quality of empathetic understanding, and while it may feel unnatural at first, my experience is that with time, it feels intuitive. If the mirroring you provide is inaccurate, don't worry. The other person will clarify and keep talking, helping both of you to better understand.

2. **Visible affirmation shows you are listening.** Sometimes "active listening" is described as physical engagement in a conversation; this can materialize in adamant head-nodding and affirmative noises. However, these same "active listening" techniques can portray impatience, as if the listener is waiting to assert his or her next response. Instead, limiting physical reactions somewhat will allow the speaker to feel as though it is okay to keep talking, that you are patient and want to hear what is being shared. Sometimes, I use the gesture of a hand on my heart when I want to empathize with someone. This helps me to avoid other more distracting gestures while still expressing my emotions.

3. **Someone needs to be talking in order for listening to happen.** One of the most valuable listening skills one can build is the ability to be with silence. Let silence be a part of the space you share with others, even if it feels uncomfortable at first. People need time to process, and you can be fully present with that reality, too — with practice. In a beautiful quote from the novel *The History of Love* by Nicole Krauss, an obituary for the character Isaac Babel reads, "When he heard music, he no longer listened to the notes, but the silences between. When he read a book, he gave himself over to the commas and semicolons, to the space after the period before the capital letter of the next sentence…When people spoke to him, he heard less and less of what they said and more and more of what they were not." In the space of the unsaid, too, resides insight and wisdom. Can we be tentative listeners to this form of communication as well?

As an assignment in the aforementioned pastoral care class, we were asked to take turns listening to one another for 45 minutes each. We were supposed to maintain full focus on the other person the entire time, using only mirroring statements while they spoke. Afterward, we reflected on the experience and evaluated our own listening skills. If you can engage in this type of deep work, I suggest it. To practice listening and to know what it feels like to be heard are both experiences that will inform the way you move through the world.

I do a much shorter version of this in my workshops, five minutes of listening to someone else. I often receive feedback that this style of communicating feels uncomfortable and unnatural. People even suggest that five minutes is way too long! My answer is always, like anything new, it takes practice and can feel a little vulnerable at first. However, seeing the other person light up when he or she feels understood is enough fuel to keep trying. I can tell you that I now use this model of listening in my own life intuitively. It's not something I do all of the time. There are many reasons to communicate, and in some situations it would seem silly. I don't need to mirror back my son's request to help him find his bookbag in the morning. However, in the countless times someone has come to me suffering — a family member struggling with addiction, a friend going through a divorce, a client whose mother is dying — I have been profoundly grateful to be able help the other person feel heard, seen, and comforted.

EMOTIONAL RISK-TAKING

Time Commitment: Varies

Frequency: Once in the next two weeks, and as desired afterward

Resources: None

Seeking connection with others is emotionally risky. Many of our most deeply rooted impulses evolve from a desire to avoid the pain of rejection. These same impulses, however, can also create alienation. The truth is, our sources of shame are just aspects of being human. We are all flawed. But in order to discover this, we have to be willing to open up to others and share what's inside.

The ways in which you find common humanity will depend upon your own tolerance for emotional risk-taking, and you can start anywhere. If you rarely share anything personal with anyone, then maybe begin by revealing something that worries you to a close, trusted friend. Notice the ways you feel uncomfortable, but also notice how the experience defies your expectations.

If you are a verbal processor like me, then there is a good chance that your close friends already know the things you struggle with. Risk will look different for you. What are the things you don't share, and why? If the reason you are hiding them is a sense of shame, there is a chance that finding someone you can confide in will provide some relief.

Commit to a strategic plan. What will you share, and with whom? After you have tried this practice once, reflect on how you can use the experience to build a tolerance for vulnerability in other situations. For example, I recently apologized to my mom when I snapped at her over something small. This made me feel quite vulnerable. Looking back, I think it was because I admitted to something that cast me in an unflattering light. Even though I felt uncomfortable, the situation is an example of how I am building a greater capacity for admitting my own negative qualities and owning them. Perhaps it is that same skill that allowed me to write this book. There are things written on these pages that I don't always share with others because they reflect poorly on me or evoke shame. However, writing an honest account that may eventually help someone else feels worth the discomfort, so it's a capacity I am willing to continue building.

In my workshops, trainings, and retreats, increasing vulnerability and practicing emotional risk-taking are some of the most valuable skills I teach. Understanding that we are not alone, that our problems are shared by those around us, is a profound gift. We are all participating in this complicated, at times overwhelming, experience of being human. It's a journey best shared.

LOVING-KINDNESS

Time Commitment: 10–15 minutes

Frequency: Once in the next two weeks, and as desired afterward

Resources: None

Optional Online Resources: Loving-Kindness Practice Video

Additional Considerations: Consider adding loving-kindness to your daily mindfulness practice. You could rotate it in every other day, or add a short loving-kindness session to the end of your usual practice.

Loving-kindness practice is a compassion-building tool used frequently in mindfulness communities. You can find many versions of this practice by searching online. I originally happened upon it when I began my own mindfulness journey with Sharon Salzberg's book *Real Happiness: The Power of Meditation: A 28-Day Program.* I found it again in the Vipassana tradition while on a 10-day silent retreat. In a Vipassana context, it was called *Metta.* I am providing one version of this practice, but feel free to try others as well, or modify this one in ways that feel natural for you.

CONNECTION

1. **Start in a comfortable and upright posture.** Take
    a few deep, centering breaths.

2. **Do a quick scan and check in with yourself.**
    What thoughts, feelings, and physical sensations are
    arising? Take a few moments to get in touch with
    your experience. As you do this, begin to rest in the
    knowledge that you, like all humans, desire health,
    happiness, and peace. Understanding this, send your-
    self these wishes:

    May I be happy. May I be healthy. May I find peace.

    Notice how it feels to send these wishes to yourself
    and repeat once again:

    May I be happy. May I be healthy. May I find peace.

3. **When you are ready, let go of this self-aware-
    ness.** Instead bring into focus the face and being of
    a person (or creature) you love. When you have this
    person in your awareness, remember that they, too,
    like you and all humans, desire health, happiness,
    and peace. Understanding this, send your loved one
    these wishes:

    May you be happy. May you be healthy. May you find peace.

Notice how it feels to send these wishes to someone you love. Repeat once again:

May you be happy. May you be healthy. May you find peace.

4. **When you are ready, let your loved one fade from your awareness.** Instead bring into focus the face and being of an acquaintance — someone you don't have a close or personal relationship with. This could be a person who works in a coffee shop you visit, or a neighbor you wave to from across the street. When this person is in your awareness, remember that they, too, like you and all humans, desire health, happiness, and peace. Understanding this, send these wishes:

    May you be happy. May you be healthy. May you find peace.

    Notice how it feels to send these wishes to someone you have only met in passing. Repeat once again:

    May you be happy. May you be healthy. May you find peace.

5. **When you are ready, let this acquaintance fade from your awareness.** Instead bring into focus the face and being of a person you struggle with. Perhaps you find it difficult to interact with this person. Maybe there is some tension in the relationship, or

the person causes you some minor annoyance. When you have him or her in your awareness, remember that this person, too, like you and all humans, desires health, happiness, and peace. Understanding this, send these wishes:

May you be happy. May you be healthy. May you find peace.

Notice how it feels to send these wishes to someone you have struggled with. Repeat once again:

May you be happy. May you be healthy. May you find peace.

6. **When you are ready, let this person fade from your awareness.** Instead bring into focus all humans and living creatures, those in your home, neighborhood, country, and world, remembering that all who live on this planet desire health, happiness, and peace. Understanding this, send these wishes:

May we be happy. May we be healthy. May we find peace.

Notice how it feels to send these wishes to all beings, and repeat:

May we be happy. May we be healthy. May we find peace.

7. **Let go of this final wish, and rest again in your own experience.** Take a few deep, centering breaths and, if you have time, reflect upon what it was like to send these wishes to yourself and others. Were there times that this practice was difficult, joyful, relieving? Approach your experience with nonjudgmental awareness and a sense of curiosity.

NARRATIVES OF INCLUSION

Time Commitment: 20–25 minutes

Frequency: Once in the next two weeks, and as desired afterward

Resources: Paper and a pen or pencil

We all have a natural inclination to seek love and connection; we also have the desire to see ourselves positively, as worthy of love. Sometimes, in order to protect our own value, we avoid seeing the ways in which we exclude others. The Narratives of Inclusion practice is built upon the idea that our "truths" and personal narratives are always inherently exclusionary, simply by nature of being human and therefore unable to have more than one perspective. It assumes that, in order to mitigate this self-focused bias, we have to be conscious of it and work to expand our perspective.

There was a time in my life when I realized that while I saw myself as an open-minded, liberal person who cared about social justice, in reality, my relationships did not reflect values of diversity and inclusion. This self-knowledge was embarrassing and even shameful for me. The specific moment that is most poignant is a difficult story to recount.

I was sitting on the patio of a coffee shop with a couple of other women. We were in the initial meetings of a recently formed book group, and there had just been a conflict about race between one of the two women with whom I was talking and someone else from our group who had already left. As we processed this experience, I looked at them both and said aloud, "I just realized that all of my friends look just like me. All of the women I am really close with are white. They all dress a certain way. They have similar education and cultural backgrounds. I think they are even a similar weight!" When I said this, the other two women looked at me with disdain.

While difficult and embarrassing, once I allowed this honest self-reflection, I took action in ways I wasn't capable of before. Some of these efforts were quite explicit — trainings, lectures, and research about bias and its impact. My most valuable action, however, was the work I did to transform my unconscious bias into conscious intention. I set the intention to notice who

I gravitated toward and to step outside of my comfort zone. I became more curious about all people, their stories and their world, how they were different from me and also similar. With this intention, my social sphere changed organically. I didn't set goals like, "I have to have a friend of X religion or race." Instead, I just became more curious, open, and cognizant of the ways I naturally gravitated to people who were like myself, and tried to avoid that tendency.

With this in mind, the following practice will help you notice the ways you gravitate toward people who are similar to you in some way or another. When you feel this tendency in yourself, pause. Notice the choices you are making and why. See whether there is another choice you could make in the moment that would be more inclusive.

For this activity, find a quiet place where you can be alone. I would suggest beginning with a short breath-focused practice to clear some mental space and facilitate focus. When you are ready, guide yourself through this narrative process at your own pace, answering each reflective question in writing, and then pausing before you move onto the next one.

1. **Mentally place yourself back in your childhood home.** You are in elementary school, in second grade. Describe your neighborhood. Was it urban, suburban, rural? Did you have neighbors who were mostly of a

similar or different race? Religion? Socio-economic status? Cultural group?

2. **Now imagine your school.** What type of student were you? Were you a high-achiever? Were you just getting by? Who were your friends? Were your friends similar to you or different from you racially, ethnically, religiously, politically, or otherwise? Who taught you? Did you identify with them as similar or different from yourself?

3. **Now imagine yourself as a teenager.** Ask yourself these same questions: What type of student were you? Were you a high-achiever? Were you just getting by? Who were your friends? Were your friends similar to you or different from you racially, ethnically, religiously, or otherwise? Who taught you? Did you identify with them as similar or different from yourself?

4. **Flash forward to today.** Describe your neighborhood. Is it rural, urban, suburban? Do you have neighbors who are of a different race? Religion? Socio-economic status? Cultural group? Political perspective? Do you regularly interact with people who are different from you?

5. **Take a moment to reflect upon your current close relationships.** Do you have close relationships with people who are different than you racially, ethnically, religiously, politically, or otherwise?

6. **Now take a moment to ask yourself the questions:** Who is missing from my story? What might I not be seeing from my one vantage point? How might my story be keeping me from recognizing someone else's truth?

7. **Once you have answered this question, then ask yourself:** How can I be intentional about owning my own story, while also creating bridges that allow me to connect with the truth of others? What would have to change in my life in order to do this?

8. **Set an intention to make one specific change in your life that will create a bridge and connect you to others.** Write this down as an "I" statement and reflect on it daily for the next week (or longer). For example:

   I will be conscious of the power I hold as a parent and the ways my child is a different type of student than I was.

   I will recognize when I am in a position of power or priv-

CONNECTION

ilege and make sure that I include the voices of others in those conversations whenever possible.

I will notice the way I react to otherness and reflect upon my internal states.

CHAPTER 16

Tools for Connection

TOOL 1: SELF-ASSESSMENT

A good starting place for thinking about interconnectedness is our own personal relationships. In what ways do you affect others? Who affects you, and how? Where do you get your emotional needs met, and is there room to grow in this area? Relationship inventories are a way to begin exploring our own rich networks in order to answer these questions.

For this relationship self-assessment, you need a blank piece of paper, which you will fold into thirds longways. Label the left column of the paper "My Network," and beneath it make a list of all of the people (or creatures) you are grateful to be connected to.

CONNECTION

After you have written your list, label the middle column of your paper "What I Receive." In this column, write down the specific qualities and experiences each person (or creature) brings to your life. For example, Jory, my teenage son, was listed in my first column. In the second column, I wrote, "laughter and new perspectives" as the gifts he brings to my life.

The third and last column will be labeled "What I Give." In this section, list the the gifts you give to the other person. In my third column I wrote that I give Jory "physical comfort, a sense of belonging, and a structured and safe environment." As his mother, these are things I try to provide.

When you have completed your relationship inventory, take a few minutes to assess your network, understanding that every relationship has its own dynamic and unique purpose.

- What positive realizations did you have in this process?
- Is there anything you want to see grow in your relationships — for example, even *more* laughter (something I think we all need)?
- How might you capitalize even further on the gifts you already give to others?

TOOL 2: SETTING AN INTENTION

We can use the power of intention to further appreciate, and perhaps even deepen, our current connections. In the self-assessment, you explored your closest personal relationships and assessed your network, perhaps not only looking for ways to grow your own gifts, but also appreciating the gifts others give you. This same exploration can be conducted for all of our relationships, including those that are fleeting. Even micro-interactions provide the opportunity to both give and receive the gifts implicit in connection. When you receive a smile, a moment of kindness, or a brief conversation, it brings a measure of joy. Conversely, you may give the gift of helpfulness, opening the door for someone or picking up and returning something they dropped. This also provides comfort to another person.

Each of these small moments could potentially go unnoticed, but with the power of intention, you can begin to see all the ways relationships impact each moment. Set an intention to notice and appreciate the myriad connection in your daily life as they unfold. Here is an example:

I will be aware of the many connections that unfold in the moments of my life, honoring and appreciating all of the ways they enrich my own existence.

At the end of each day, take a few moments to reflect on your intention, asking yourself questions such as:

- Whom did I receive gifts from? What did they give me, and how did I show appreciation?
- Whom did I give gifts to, and how were those gifts received by others?
- What was the quality of the attention I gave to my relationships today?

TOOL 3: CONNECTING WITH MENTORS

The field of connection and compassion has one particular researcher who has influenced my work and perspective on this topic considerably. Brené Brown, researcher of vulnerability and shame and explorer of the whole-hearted, cannot be recommended enough. Study her work and the others outlined here with my highest recommendation.

Brené Brown's TEDTalk "The power of vulnerability." There is a quote I frequently share from this talk by Brown: "…vulnerability is the core of shame and fear and our struggle for worthiness, but it appears that it's also the birthplace of joy, of creativity, of belonging, of love." In essence, she argues that with vulnerability, we have deeper relationships, a higher quality of life, and

MYTHS OF BEING HUMAN

more meaning and purpose. Without it, meaningful relationships are impossible, our quality of life decreases, and we move listlessly through our existence. This 15-minute video changed the way I view the world of relationships.

Brené Brown's second TEDTalk, "Listening to shame." One important thing Brown discusses in this talk is the importance of including men in conversations about vulnerability. Society shames males for showing emotions, and it begins at a young age. And yet, men and boys have all the same emotional needs as females. This major problem in our society needs to be considered seriously. All humans carry something heavy. Often, however, there is no safe place for males to put these things down and rest in the care of others.

Julian Treasure's TEDTalk "5 ways to listen better." This 8-minute talk offers practical advice to improve our listening, a skill Treasure describes as our ability to "make meaning from sound." Among the tools he suggests are finding three minutes of silence daily, practicing gratitude for sounds, trying to pick out different parts of a soundscape, and choosing a "listening stance" to embody while in conversations. Most powerfully, he states, "Conscious listening always creates understanding." He suggests listening is the path to greater peace.

CONNECTION

Matthew Lieberman's book *Social: Why Our Brains Are Wired to Connect*. Lieberman's book provides an evolutionary and scientific look at how we are meant to connect with one another. A social neuroscientist, Lieberman shares and explains research supporting interconnection and compassion as the default and necessary human state.

MYTHS OF BEING HUMAN

Conclusion: Connecting With What Matters

WE DON'T NEED TO WAIT UNTIL THINGS FALL APART

On the pages of this book, I explore my own shifts in thinking and action. These shifts happened due to personal trauma. In my case, I didn't truly wake up to what was important in life until circumstances forced me to do so. But does this always need to be the case?

In every moment, we have a personal choice. Each moment, we can choose to wake up to what matters or continue creating lives based upon what others value. I was recently listening to an interview with author and C-level executive of Facebook, Sheryl Sandberg, and her friend Adam Grant, a psychologist and author. The interview focused on Sandberg's journey after the unexpected death of her husband in 2015, and how Grant helped her recover by sharing the science of growth through trauma.

While no one welcomes trauma, science does suggest that we can learn something from post-traumatic growth. Sandberg and Grant pose a challenge in the interview: Can we experience the growth some find through devastating personal circumstances in other ways? Can pre-traumatic growth happen if we maintain a heightened sense of gratitude for the here and now? I hope this book will help others live within this space of wonder and awe, before having to encounter life-transforming circumstances.

Building that type of life is about the specifics, the small choices we make moment-to-moment. Do I look my children in the eyes when they tell me "good morning"? Do I stop to give my husband a kiss as I head out the door? Each small decision is a microcosm of the lives we lead. Or, in the words of Annie Dillard (as cited in Tippett, 2017), "How we spend our days is, of course, how we spend our lives."

So what matters to you? What values do you aspire to put at the center of your life? How you answer these questions will determine the practices and the extent of usage you sustain after reading this book. These final thoughts are intended to help you dive more deeply into these questions and build the four paths into your life in meaningful, personal ways.

There are three sections to help plan a sustained journey:

1. **Connect with your values.** Determine what's most important, and then decide which tools will help you stay focused on those priorities.

2. **Plan your pause.** Set aside time to reflect, make meaning, and recharge as you live a values-based life.

3. **Hone your discernment skills.** Make decisions based upon what matters to you.

Before I go further, I want to pause and address the dichotomy between the concept of "managing" stress but also being encouraged to embrace it. I have previously mentioned Kelly McGonigal as a reference for some of the research in this book. In *The Upside of Stress: Why Stress is Good for You and How to Get Good At It*, she encourages individuals to chase meaning and embrace connection as tools to mitigate the negative impacts of stress. According to McGonigal, there are certain criteria which create negative emotional and physical health consequences in times of challenge. They include: personal inadequacy, isolation, powerlessness, and loss of meaning. When circumstances evoke these types of responses, stress can have negative consequences. Therefore, anything you can do to feel more adequate, to become more connected, and to create more meaning from your stressors, will mitigate any and all negative impacts you may have experienced otherwise. According to McGonigal, for people whose lives are full of meaning, purpose, connection, and personal adequacy, they experience *no* negative impacts from stress.

All of this is true, *and* there are times when life knocks us on our asses. As stated previously, knowing that meaning may come later doesn't stop the pain. Pain is a reality of hardship. We are all going to have traumatic stress that at times feels unmanageable. This is just life. During these times, a temporary sense of personal inadequacy and loss of self-efficacy may be unavoidable. However, this doesn't have to last forever. Just knowing about post-traumatic growth, combined with planning for pauses, can help.

Stress is a "yes, and" experience. *Yes*, too much of the "bad" stress is not good for us. *And* there are benefits from even the worst of times, even when pain is so overwhelming we are not sure whether we can survive. I say this from experience.

Stress, like all things, is best managed from what Buddhists call "the middle way," or the path between two extremes. One end of the extreme is our desire to completely avoid the reality of difficult emotions and repress anything that feels unpleasant. On the other end of the extreme is our tendency to get swept into overwhelming feelings of inadequacy, doubt, and fear in times of difficulty and to let those feelings rule our decision-making and self-perception.

Stress is both unavoidable and also something we can learn to live with in a healthy way (most of the time). The next three sections are intended to help you operate within the middle path — a path focused on knowing what is important and sometimes being uncomfortable in order to obtain it. A path for remaining healthy and whole, even when the discomfort comes along.

Connect With Your Values

When humans lack a sense of purpose, hopelessness often develops. Conversely, a purpose-filled life is full of meaning, even when things are difficult. Determining our most important values can help to facilitate the latter — a meaning-filled, purposeful life. The following activity is intended to help you determine your own values. You will then use these values to plan the tools you want to sustain in daily life.

Begin by downloading the "Personal Values Card Sort" by Miller, Baca, Mathews, and Wilbourne available on the Book Resources page online; you can download the Connect With Your Values worksheet from there to use with the activity as well.

1. **Print and cut out the cards.** Separate out the title cards: *Important to Me*, *Very Important to Me*, and *Not Important to Me*.

2. **Separate all of the remaining cards.** Make three piles underneath each of the title cards. You will have one stack of *Important* values, one stack of *Very Important* values, and one stack of *Not Important* values.

3. **Assess the three piles.** Set aside the *Important to Me* and *Not Important to Me* pile. Look again at each card in the *Very Important to Me* pile and try to choose your top three values. (Some people find this step to be challenging, but it is a necessary part of the process. If it is helpful, begin by narrowing the pile to the top five to ten before determining the top three.)

4. **For each of your top three values, answer the following questions:**

    - What does this value mean to you?
    - How does your life currently reflect this value?
    - What choices could you make to further live through this value?

5. **Once you have answered these questions, consider which path(s) would be most helpful to fulfilling your top three values.** This will determine which practices you want to adopt more permanently. For example, one of my personal values is wisdom. I know that in order to be wise, I have to take time to

clear my mind and gain perspective. Formal mindfulness practice helps me to do this, so I choose to continue using it because it supports a value that is important to me. Here is a quick overview of the paths and tools that you may choose to continue implementing:

- **Path of Mindfulness:** Mindfulness "On the Cushion," activities from your Rejuvenation Map, and Shinrin Yoku (see practices in Chapter 3)
- **Path of Gratitude:** Beautiful Moments, Saying It Out Loud, and Recognizing and Connecting with the Suffering of Others (see practices in Chapter 7)
- **Path of Growth:** Reframing Challenges, Finding Guidance Within, and Cultivating Forgiveness (see practices in Chapter 11)
- **Path of Connection:** Mindful Listening, Emotional Risk-Taking, Loving-Kindness and Narratives of Inclusion (see practices in Chapter 15)

6. **Having determined which tools you want to continue using, write a statement connecting your value to the practice.** Commit to when and how you will use it. For example, *I will practice 20 minutes of formal mindfulness daily because it helps me to make wise*

decisions. Keep these statements where you can see and reflect on them regularly.

As a final note, this activity is not intended to create lifelong rules and boundaries for which practices you will use. Certain paths may be more important at different times in your life, making some practices more useful than others. Connecting those that are useful to your values is about understanding *why* you've made this choice for how to spend your time.

Knowing what is important to me has helped with more than building a practice. I literally build my life around my values. It sounds obvious, but there is a surprising lack of attention in society on being purposeful with our time in ways unrelated to productivity.

Knowing my values has also helped me to understand what doesn't matter. As an example, another important value to me is family. I want to be a good wife, mother, daughter, and sister. When I went through business coaching a few months ago, I was asked to state what I needed in the categories of work, personal life, money, and work environment. These all seem like important things, but experience has taught me that if I don't have my personal life in order, then everything else falls apart. Family is an influential and crucial component of getting my personal life right. Because I knew this clearly and decisively, giving up items in the other categories came more easily.

I realized that I had to say no to things I sometimes wanted in order to say yes to the things that mattered most, like my role as a wife and mother.

Plan Your Pause

Regardless of which values you want to live through, rejuvenation is necessary. We all have the need to recalibrate during times of stress, and it helps to have tools for this. You have already discovered some of these personalized resources when you completed your Rejuvenation Map. There are also certain practices from this book that may be helpful. For example, formal mindfulness practice, Shinrin Yoku, and loving-kindness meditation are all intended to facilitate more inner quiet, which is a natural stress reliever.

Take a moment to reflect on which of these tools (either from chapters on practices or your Rejuvenation Map) have been most helpful when you needed to reset. In other words, what facilitates your ability to calm, slow down, and gain perspective? Take a moment to write down your thoughts on this question.

Now that you have an idea of which tools are most helpful, remember that you can use them in two ways. First, they can be preventative medicine. There are certain things I try to do either every day or most days, like yoga and formal mindfulness practice. Taking time for these activities keeps me mentally healthy. Your pauses might also be used as treatment in times of challenge. When we created Rejuvenation Maps, you identified your stress tells. These are physical, emotional, and behavioral symptoms that occur when you reach your capacity for managing obstacles. The tools that help you create pause are especially helpful when these symptoms occur and may prevent the use of more negative coping mechanisms. In addition to the ones already mentioned, I also use Yoga Nidra[5] during times of tension. Yoga Nidra invokes deep states of relaxation, so it is particularly helpful when stress is overwhelming. I also seek out more physical contact with others at these times. I ask Jory and Jamey for hugs, read books with Sawyer while snuggling in bed, and spend more time playing with my dog Tucker. Physical touch has been shown through research to have therapeutic

---

5 Yoga Nidra is a sometimes called "Yogic Sleep," but it is intended to put participants in a state between waking and sleeping, leading to a very deep relaxation. I first found this practice when I was attending a Y12SR (Yoga for Twelve-Step Recovery) leadership training. To practice Yoga Nidra, I lay in Corpse Pose (or Savasana) with my knees elevated by a pillow and a towel covering my eyes. I then put on headphones and drift into a deep state of relaxation while listening to an audio recording for thirty minutes or so. There are many versions of Yoga Nidra. The one I use most frequently can be found on gaia.com, an online resource that charges about $10.00 a month. There are free versions available elsewhere, too.

benefits, so I know this is time well spent.

Lastly, when possible in times of stress, I extend (or at least sustain) the amount of time I spend on formal mindfulness practice whenever possible. It is *highly* tempting to leave my practice behind when I am feeling overwhelmed. It is actually painful for me to sit and be with my own thoughts and emotions when they feel like they are spinning out of control. However, I know that if I can slow down my thinking and response time by even a small degree, I will be much better off in the long run. When I am smart and strong enough to realize this, it pays off every time.

Does this mean that I always do what's best for me? I wish that were true, but just like all humans everywhere, I make bad choices when I reach my maximum capacity and feel overwhelmed. The pinnacle of these choices is something that happened to me recently, which I am calling "The Hilliard Incident." (Hilliard is a suburb of Columbus, Ohio.)

The story of The Hilliard Incident begins on a Monday. I had been quite busy over the last few weeks with meetings and obligations, and this particular Monday was no exception. I was an hour outside of town, meeting with a potential new client, and I was supposed to leave to pick up Sawyer by 3:30. At 5:30, I was still an hour away from home. Fortunately, I texted Jamey earlier in the afternoon and he was able to take care of my family obligations. Still, I had a long drive ahead of me and would no longer be able to prepare dinner for my family (something I do most weekdays).

The trek back to Columbus began a little before 6:00, and about halfway there, I smelled something burning and quickly realized I had a flat tire. After calling our roadside assistance service to help and then waiting for them to arrive, I didn't make it home for bedtime, let alone dinner.

I had four presentations in the morning starting at 7:30 a.m., and I still had work to do. After kissing a sleeping Sawyer on the head, I got out my laptop and started working. This was a problem. I rarely work in the evenings after my kids and husband get home. In addition, I had skipped my evening meditation and had not exercised at all that day. I looked at my husband before I went to bed, and said, "This isn't good. I need to slow down."

If only I had listened to my own advice.

The next day, I was up at 5:45 a.m. and out the door an hour later. I needed to make it to the location of my four-presentation series in Hilliard, a school district I was building a new relationship with. When I pulled my car up to Darby Middle School, the building in which I was presenting, a student was helpful enough to help me find the room…except we couldn't find it, even together. Eventually, I stopped a teacher and asked her where it was. I told her I was there for the all-day professional development in Hilliard.

"Are you sure you are at the right Darby Middle School?" she asked

"Is there more than one?" I said.

"You are in Westerville, not Hilliard."

It was now 7:30. I would not be making it to my first presentation.

Back in my car, I put the correct Darby Middle School into Google Maps. It was 36 minutes away. This is when I entered a state of panic. I called my contact in the correct city and left an extremely apologetic message, "I will be there as soon as possible, but I will not be able to present the first session. I am so, so sorry."

With hands still shaking, I left the parking lot and began the 36-minute drive. It wasn't long, however, before bright lights were flashing in my rearview — I was being pulled over. After stopping my car on a side street, the police officer walked up to my window. "Do you know why I pulled you over?" he asked.

"No. No. I am so, so sorry. I am really late for a presentation I am supposed to be giving. I went to the wrong location."

"You were going 35 in a school zone."

"I am really sorry. I am just in a crazy panic. I had no idea. I am just trying to get to this presentation."

"What time does your presentation start?"

"7:30."

"Well, you're obviously not going to make it, so there

is no reason to be speeding." The clock said 7:45. The officer went to write me a ticket.

It was in this moment that I actually lost my mind. I remembered that he didn't know I had a *second* presentation beginning at 8:30. My GPS said that if I left in the next 15 minutes, I would still make it. So I took a deep breath, put my hands up, and got out of my car.

"Sir…" I said as I walked toward his vehicle, "is it okay for me to be out of my car?"

"No," he replied, "Get back in your car."

"Ok," I acquiesced, hands still in the air, now walking backward toward my own vehicle, "I just wanted to tell you I have another presentation, and if I leave in the next 15 minutes, I can still make it."

"Stop worrying about your presentations and get back in your car!"

I returned to my driver's side, and called my contact again.

"Did you get my voicemail?" I asked.

"I was just listening to it when you called," she said.

"I just wanted to tell you that I should be able to make it for the second presentation…If the cop that pulled me over lets me go in the next 15 minutes."

"Oh, God." she said. "Just be careful. Keep me updated."

I got off the phone and the adrenaline racing through my body turned to emotional upheaval. I began crying. As the police officer handed me a $170.00 ticket, I turned away, still sobbing.

He did let me go, and I eventually made it to my second presentation. When I got there, I actually used this story as the introduction. How could I not? It perfectly illustrates what happens when we refuse to slow down.

I knew I had been over-scheduling myself even leading up to that Monday. My seven-year-old had asked me a few days before, "Mommy, why you always leaving us hanging?" This was his way of saying I had been gone too frequently during times that were normally designated for family. To further my over-scheduling problems, I had also started breaking my work/home boundary, sitting on my laptop when I should have been spending time with people who matter to me. Compounding this, I stopped taking care of myself. I didn't take time to pause and recalibrate. Instead, I gave in to my urge to go faster and faster.

All of this led me to the point where my adrenaline-addled brain started making some truly poor decisions. I didn't double-check the address in my GPS to make sure it was correct. *I got out of my car and approached a police officer after being pulled over.* Clearly, I wasn't thinking straight. Even though the things I was doing were important, they were not more important than my health and well-being. They were certainly not more important than the time I spend with my family.

When I tell this story now, I am keenly aware of how much worse it could have been. The choices I made put me and others in danger. This is the risk taken when we resist the signs to slow down and allow the urges to push harder and go faster take over.

The incidents that occurred over those two days had a lasting impact on me in many ways. For one, it took me a week to feel better. I had run myself down so much, that depression and exhaustion set in. Second of all, I realized the true cost of not heeding my own advice. It was a wake-up call to reassess the ways I take care of myself, even and especially when I don't feel like it. Lastly, the situation forced me to evaluate how I spend my time. I realized that as my business continued to grow, I needed to have a clear process for making decisions about my life and work, which is a perfect segue into the next section, honing your discernment skills.

Hone Your Discernment Skills

Mindfulness creates a space that allows us to make different decisions. However, it doesn't solve the problem of *how* those decisions should be made and *what* those decisions should be. Certainly, as we become more mindful, our self-awareness builds, which is a great benefit to our decision-making abilities. At the same time, we still need to put forth conscious attention in order to protect what we value.

As an entrepreneur, I am in charge of my own schedule more than most people. This is a benefit, to be sure. If I decide I need a long hike and I have time available, no one tells me no. At the same time, I am continually making decisions about how to best spend my time, which can be a little exhausting. While still in the process of figuring out how to do this well, using what matters most to me in order to build the life I want is getting easier. Being clear on values helps with this, but then I have to make decisions that support them.

I recently facilitated a workshop activity on setting personal intentions for a season. While planning the activity, I wrote my own as an example, and focused on this exact thing: making decisions that reflect what is most important to me. Below are the steps to creating your own Values-Based Intentions and Goals, along with my personal examples. (You can download a Values-Based Intentions and Goal Setting worksheet on the Book Resources page.)

1. **Determine your goal-based intention**[6]: Revisit your values, and set a goal-based intention based

---

6 Goal-based intentions are intended to reflect the result you want. Implementation intentions are what you need to do to get there.

upon what matters to you. You can use the stem:

My schedule and activities will reflect my values of...

Here is my example:

My schedule will reflect my values of quality, family, and self-care.

2. **Determine obstacles you might face:** Consider barriers to living through these values. Try not to be abstract, and instead focus on behavioral obstacles that you have control over. For example, checking social media and email unnecessarily is a habit that keeps me from doing quality work. Stopping this habit is a tangible change that is within my power. Here are obstacles to my goal-based intention:

   • Social media, email, and other time wasters
   • Obligations bleeding into family and self-care time
   • My aversion to self-care when I am stressed

3. **Set an implementation intention to address each of your obstacles.** For each obstacle you have identified, set an intention that reflects the process you will use to avoid the behavior. For

example, I wrote an implementation intention to help me avoid checking social media and email. When I connect the habit to its detrimental impact on my value of creating quality work, I better understand that the momentary gain I get from the distraction may not be worth the cost. I may even put a note on my computer that reminds me how every time I check something else while working on a project, I suffer 15 to 20 minutes of decreased cognitive capacity on my main task because of attentional residue.[7] Here are my implementations intentions to address each obstacle:

Obstacle 1: Social media

Implementation Intention: When I feel tempted to spend time on social media or checking my email, I will remind myself how each time I do this, I undermine my value of quality and create attentional residue.

Obstacle 2: Obligations

Implementation Intention: When I am considering a new

---

7 Attentional residue is a concept outlined in the book *Deep Work* by Cal Newport. When we try to multitask, we are actually switching between tasks. As our attention moves from one task to the other, it creates a task-related "residue" that lasts fifteen to twenty minutes. Our cognitive capacities are lowered for this amount of time as part of our brain is still attending to the other task.

commitment, I will pause before responding, add it to my to-do list, and come back to it later when I have thought about how it reflects my values.

Obstacle 3: Aversion to Self-Care
Implementation Intention: When I want to avoid self-care, I will remind myself of "The Hilliard Incident."

4. **Determine any other actions you think might be helpful.** Besides overcoming obstacles, there may be other actions that can contribute to your ability to make values-based decisions. Consider what else might help you meet your goal-based intention. Here is my list of other helpful actions:

    • Systems of organization that help me set priorities
    • Keeping clear and consistent boundaries between work and home life

5. **Write at least one or more implementation intentions for each helpful action.** For example, in "The Hilliard Incident," one of my initial problems was over-scheduling. I was exerting poor control over my calendar, letting my days be determined by the values of others instead of my personal values. Because of this, I was feeling frazzled before any

of the more challenging events even started, and it interrupted my ability to care for myself. In the end, I suffered, and the work I was trying to do did as well. Knowing this, I took the suggestion of a fellow mindfulness teacher, Juan Alvarez, and wrote the following intention related to scheduling, "When I am considering a new commitment, I will pause before responding, add it to my to-do list, and come back to it later when I have thought about how it reflects my values." Here are my other implementation intentions related to helpful actions:

Helpful Action: Systems of Organization
Implementation Intention: I will review my calendar daily and plan my activities based upon my values, minimizing distractions.

Helpful Action: Systems of Organization
Implementation Intention: I will add items that require attention to a list and then do them when I have allotted time (as opposed to getting swept up in email).

Helpful Action: Keeping Clear Boundaries
Implementation Intention: At the end of the day, I will review my to-do list, adding and subtracting as needed. Then, I will shut my computer down and put it out of eyesight before I pick up the kids.

CONNECTING WITH WHAT MATTERS

This activity is merely the beginning of a much longer process of making the small (and large) decisions that form a life. As our lives change, our values may also shift. Intentions such as these are simply tools to gain perspective on what matters to you now, so you can make decisions accordingly.

Upon reflection, I realized that my values were a little mundane. My most important things weren't to change the world or to make a contribution to humanity. Instead, they were about caring for myself and others while doing quality work. I think at many points in my life, these goals would have seemed like too little. As I have learned to reflect on my own inner compass, however, I have found that what I can actually control and what truly makes my life balanced and whole is grounded in the simple things. Simple, but maybe not so easy. Setting these personal intentions helps me stay in the here and now, but it still remains a challenge. I have a tendency to swim in the abstract and the conceptual, to have idealistic dreams of what could be rather than simply living. As a teacher of mine once aptly reminded me, however, "all the work we can do is only 20 feet from us." While I certainly get to make choices about what is in that space, to assume anything grander is outside of my control and takes me away from the work right in front of me.

Final Thoughts

A clear understanding of what matters to you is important, but it doesn't provide all of the answers. There are times in our lives when we have to listen a little harder to know what is needed in the moment. Inner quiet is another, and sometimes the best, resource for honing discernment. It creates a pause, and at the same time, it is also a tool for connecting with our intuition. This is where I, personally, leave the door open for mystery in my life.

The poem "Clearing" by Martha Postlethwaite uses the metaphor of a clearing in a forest to describe how inner quiet can help us to connect with our intuitiveness. With her permission, here are the words she shares,

create a clearing
in the dense forest
of your life
and wait there
patiently until the song
that is yours alone to sing
falls into your open cupped hands.

Somewhere within each of us, there is a quiet space that speaks to who we are, what we truly need, what unique gifts we each bring to this world.

CONNECTING WITH WHAT MATTERS

We live in a world of distraction, and simply being human means our lives are complicated. If we do not clear a space for ourselves within, we could end up lost and wandering, looking for the elusive "right answer" based wholly on external cues. The solution to this is not more action, but instead cultivating a space of internal stillness. In that stillness, if we listen closely and with an open mind and heart, our intuition can be a guiding force that helps us find ourselves in the thick of life.

Through noticing more deeply, through learning not to resist and instead to welcome, I did indeed discover my own song. Like music, my intuition is sometimes loud and sometimes quiet, sometimes full of beauty and sometimes forewarning. Always present if I can be patient, if I can stop, if I can listen.

I can say that there are some things I know about life now. Things that come from that inner quiet, listening, and allowing. What I know isn't much. It is only this: that life is magical. That it is full of dark beauty and light so bright we must avert our eyes.

I know that we each have a song. That our song moves us in moments that are powerful and overwhelming. That other moments, it's a melody so soft we strain our ears to hear and barely catch what's carried on the wind.

I know we each have refuge. We have refuge in one another and refuge in ourselves. We find hope in gentle touches and strength in silent moments.

I know I am grateful. Grateful for beauty. For darkness. For light. For otherness and inwardness. I am grateful for all of it.

I know that my life is only a fragment. A tiny particle of something almost ethereal. It will be here and then it will be gone.

I know that my life is also powerful. That the traces I leave behind will ripple further into the future than my consciousness can even comprehend.

I know that my voice, on this page, is not my own. It is the voice of ancestors and contemporaries who shape my perspective. It is the voice of billions of atoms, energy, and movement, temporarily held in this form.

These are the things that I know. These words are my effort to share what I know. To connect with billions of atoms, with contemporaries I will never meet. I am with you now. As you read these words, I am here.

Epilogue

I am typing now with fingers numb and stiff from a morning walk in the cold, fall air with my dog, Tucker; leaves continue to dance to the ground outside my window as the trees prepare for winter. Last night, I received the book cover from my designer, and no surprise — the prominent feature is a tree.

What I have learned from all of this, the takeaway, has everything to do with trees. Above the surface of the earth, they live solitary lives, weathering the seasons of death and rebirth year after year alone. More than once, their seeming loneliness has been the impetus for my reaching hand to pause, palm to bark, pondering what it must be like to live this way.

In a talk I planned after writing this book, however,

I began to research the lives of trees under the surface of the soil. The truth is, while they *look* like separate individuals, their root systems deep within the ground are always communicating, giving warnings of danger or changes in the environment, and sharing resources like carbon dioxide and nutrients needed to grow.

The reality is, while they may seem alone, they are actually an intimate community; they need one another to thrive.

We humans are like this. While the illusion of our separateness continues to be pervasive, our biology and human nature require rich connection much like the trees — even if that fact isn't always apparent on the surface of things.

Especially right now, in this time and place in history, there are many people living out a different reality — one that creates suffering, divisiveness, and disconnection.

I have been fortunate enough to see through my work what happens when people are given permission to do otherwise, however. There is another, parallel story. A story of what happens when individuals and communities live out of deep connection in our most public lives.

A few days ago, only weeks after finishing the text of *Myths*, I sat down and wrote an outline for my next book; it took me twenty minutes. Having more time in this work, I have seen the impact of living differently in community. I look forward to continuing the journey.

If you enjoyed this book, please write an Amazon review. Your words of support are invaluable to independent publishers like the author who rely on readers like you for their work to flourish.

MYTHS OF BEING HUMAN

Supplemental Resource: Weekly Checklist

You can use this resource to plan time to complete the activities each week.

Week 1, Mindfulness
- Read Path 1: Mindfulness
- Complete self-assessment and set intentions (15 minutes)
- Formal mindfulness practice and reflect on intentions (10–15 minutes daily)
- Create Rejuvenation Map (20 minutes)

Week 2, Mindfulness
- Formal mindfulness practice and reflect on intentions (10–15 minutes daily)
- Use tools from Rejuvenation Map (as needed)
- Shinrin Yoku (20 minutes)

Week 3, Gratitude
- Read Path 2: Gratitude
- Complete self-assessment and set intentions (15 minutes)
- Formal mindfulness practice and reflect on intentions (10–15 minutes daily)
- Beautiful Moments (5 minutes daily)

Week 4, Gratitude
- Formal mindfulness practice and reflect on

intentions (10–15 minutes daily)
- Beautiful Moments (5 minutes daily)
- Say It Out Loud (5 minutes)
- Recognizing and Connecting with Others' Suffering (24 hours)

Week 5, Growth
- Read Path 3: Growth
- Complete self-assessment and set intentions (15 minutes)
- Formal mindfulness practice and reflect on intentions (10–15 minutes daily)
- Reframing Challenges (15 minutes)

Week 6, Growth
- Formal mindfulness practice and reflect on intentions (10–15 minutes daily)
- Finding Guidance Within (15–20 minutes)
- Cultivating Forgiveness (20 minutes)

Week 7, Connection
- Read Path 4: Connection
- Complete self-assessment and set intentions (15 minutes)
- Formal mindfulness practice and/or loving-kindness practice and reflect on intentions (10–15 minutes daily)

- Mindful listening (time frame will vary)

Week 8, Connection
- Formal mindfulness practice and/or loving-kindness practice and reflect on intentions (10–15 minutes daily)
- Emotional Risk-Taking (time frame will vary)
- Narratives of Inclusion (20–25 minutes)

Week 9, Sustaining Practice
- Read the Conclusion
- Connect with your Values (30 minutes)
- Plan Your Pause (15 minutes)
- Hone Your Discernment Skills (ongoing)

Acknowledgments

There are many folks who contributed to the creation of *Myths of Being Human*, many of whom are cited on these pages. First and foremost, I want to thank my husband, Jamey Fauque, without whom I never would have started writing this book. It was his encouragement at every major juncture that kept me moving forward, and his suggestion that led me to begin this project in the first place.

Thank you, Jamey, for letting me share our story in all its beauty and all its difficulty. Thank you for being my partner and teaching me what love is.

Thank you to my beautiful children. Jory, you are truly the lifelong man in my life. Since I was eighteen years old, you have brought me comfort in times of pain and inspired me over and over again with your courage and your incredible heart. Sawyer — for your laughter and your inspirational joy and creativity which found their way to these pages many times, I am grateful. The two of you have helped me learn what matters, and you remind me again and again each day.

I want to thank the friends and family who helped me to find myself in the midst of pain and turmoil. Harmony Norman; Melissa Allen; my mom and dad, Sharon and Mark Lust; brother, Robert Lust; and my sister, Jen Kemper. Each of you stood by me in profound ways when life was falling apart. I would never have made it to who I am today without your continued love and support.

I also want to thank the mentors and contributors not mentioned on these pages. Robin Holland, the teacher who encouraged the project that began this work three years ago. You were one of my first readers, and without you this book would not have existed. Other readers I would like to thank include my friend and partner-in-crime Autumn Theodore; I love you girl. Thanks also to Leah Alexander and Catharine Hannay who provided feedback on drafts.

I would like to thank my mentor David Hett for helping me in the times of greatest difficulty mentioned in this book. You gave me the confidence to see myself as a new kind of teacher and to know I could trust myself to always do what was needed in each moment.

I would also like to thank my editor, Andrea Clute. You helped me to articulate and hone my vision, introduced me to the appropriate use of the em dash, and made me get comfortable with ending sentences with a preposition. This is your book, too!

Lastly, I would like to thank my designer, Kelley Engelbrecht, who graciously offered her many talents and gifts to make this book a reality. Kelley, your vision and caring turned a manuscript into a piece of art.

End Notes

SECTION 1: MINDFULNESS

Chapter 2: The Path Toward Mindfulness

36 learned patterns of response: Graham, L. (2013). *Bouncing back: Rewiring your brain for maximum resilience and well-being.* Novato, CA: New World Library.

37 the voice in our minds: Singer, M. (2007). *The untethered soul: The journey beyond yourself.* Oakland, CA: New Harbinger Publications and Noetic Books.

38 emotions are key to our ability to function: Pontin, J. (interviewer) & Damasio A. (interviewee). (2014, June). *The importance of feelings.* Retrieved from https://www.technologyreview.com/s/528151/the-importance-of-feelings/

38 studying patients with damage to the brain's emotional regulators: Damasio, A. (2011, Mar.). *The quest to understand consciousness* [Video File]. Retrieved from https://www.ted.com/talks/antonio_damasio_the_quest_to_understand_consciousness

40 how "mind wandering" affects happiness: Killingsworth, M. (2011, Nov.). *Want to be happier? Stay in the moment* [Video File].

END NOTES

Retrieved from https://www.ted.com/talks/matt_killingsworth_ want_to_be_happier_stay_in_the_moment?language=en

41 neuroplasticity . . . "experience-dependent" plasticity: Storr, W. (2015, Nov.). *The brain's miracle superpowers of self-improvement.* Retrieved from http://www.bbc.com/future/story/20151123-the-brains-miracle-superpowers-of-self-improvement

41 increased cortical thickness: Lazar, S., Kerr, C., Wasserman, R., Gray, J., Greve, D., Treadway, M., McGarvey, M., Quinn, B., Dusek, J., Benson, H., Rauch, S., Moore, C., & Fischl, B. (2005). Meditation experience is associated with increased cortical thickness. *Neuroreport.* 16(17), 1893-1897. Retrieved from https://www.ncbi. nlm.nih.gov/pmc/articles/PMC1361002/

42 increased gray matter in brain areas: Hölzel, B. K., Carmody, J., Vangel, M., Congleton, C., Yerramsetti, S. M., Gard, T., & Lazar, S. W. (2011). Mindfulness practice leads to increases in regional brain gray matter density. *Psychiatry Research: Neuroimaging.* 191(1), 36-43. Retrieved from http://doi.org/10.1016/j.pscychresns.2010.08.006

42 benefits of mindfulness for therapy: Davis, D. & Hayes, J. (2011). What are the benefits of mindfulness? A practice review of psychotherapy-related research. *Psychotherapy.* 48(2), 198-208. Retrieved from https://www.apa.org/pubs/journals/features/pst-48-2-198.pdf

42 a tool for mitigating the effects of implicit bias: Staats, C., Capatosto, K. Wright, R. & Jackson, V. (2016). *State of the science: Implicit bias review 2016 edition.* Retrieved from http://kirwaninstitute. osu.edu/wp-content/uploads/2016/07/implicit-bias-2016.pdf

Chapter 3: Mindfulness Practices

49 thoughts as clouds in the sky: Salzberg, S. (2011). *Real happiness: The power of meditation: A 28-day program.* New York, NY: Workman Publishing Company.

50 In your response lies your growth: *Alleged quote "between a stimulus and a response."* Retrieved from http://www.viktorfrankl.org/e/ quote_stimulus.html

53 correlations between diminished cognitive performance and economic hardship: Mani, A., Mullainathan, S., Shafir, E., & Zhao, J. (2013). Poverty impedes cognitive function. *Science.* 341(6149), 976-980. Retrieved from https://doi.org/10.1126/science.1238041

53 can be generalized to scarcity in any important resource, including time: Vedantam, S. (interviewer) & Mullainathan, S. (interviewee). (2014). *How scarcity trap affects our thinking, behavior.* Retrieved from http://www.npr.org/2014/01/02/259082836/ how-scarcity-mentaly-affects-our-thinking-behavior

END NOTES

54 "Why Mindfulness is a Superpower: An Animation": [Happify]. (2015). *Why mindfulness is a superpower: An animation* [Video File]. Retrieved from https://www.youtube.com/watch?v=w6T02g5hnT4

57 any time you are thinking about something other than what you are doing: Killingsworth, *Want to be happier? Stay in the moment.* (see end note for page 40)

64 Time in nature . . . with physical health benefits: U.S. Department of Agriculture. *Health and wellness benefits of spending time in nature.* Retrieved from https://www.fs.fed.us/pnw/about/ programs/gsv/pdfs/health_and_wellness.pdf

64 Restorative factors, such as our perception of natural environments: Kaplan, S. (1995). The restorative benefits of nature: Toward an integrative framework. *Journal of Environmental Psychology.* 15, 169-182. Retrieved from http://willsull.net/resources/ KaplanS1995.pdf

65 40-page guide available for download at Shinrin-Yoku.org: Clifford, M. (2013). *A little handbook of shinrin yoku.* Retrieved from http://www.shinrin-yoku.org/resources.html

Chapter 4: Tools for Mindfulness

66 Five Facet Mindfulness Questionnaire: *Five facet mindfulness questionnaire.* Retrieved from https://goamra.org/wp-content/

uploads/2014/06/FFMQ_full.pdf

69 Tara Brach's podcast, *Tara Brach*: Brach, T. *Tara brach.* Retrieved from https://itunes.apple.com/us/podcast/tara-brach/id265264862?mt=2

70 *Real Happiness: The Power of Meditation*: Salzberg, *Real happiness: The power of meditation: A 28-day program.* (see end note for page 49)

70 Dan Siegel's book *Mindsight*: Siegel, D. (2010). *Mindsight: The new science of personal transformation.* New York, NY: Bantam Books, an Imprint of Random House Publishing.

SECTION 2: GRATITUDE

Chapter 6: The Path Toward Gratitude

82 there are good things in the world . . . sources of good as outside of ourselves: Emmons, R. (2010). *Why gratitude is good.* Retrieved from http://greatergood.berkeley.edu/article/item/why_gratitude_is_good

82 natural inclination to pay more attention, for longer, to negative stimuli: Baumeister, R., Bratslavsky, E., Finkenauer, C., & Vohs, K. (2001). Bad is stronger than good. *Review of General Psychology.* 5(4), 323-370. Retrieved from http://psycnet.apa.org/doiLanding?doi=10.1037%2F1089-2680.5.4.323

END NOTES

83 awareness of threats better allowed the human species to survive: Vaish, A., Grossmann, T., & Woodward, A. (2008). Not all emotions are created equal: The negativity bias in social-emotional development. *Psychological Bulletin.* 134(3), 383-403. Retrieved from https://www.ncbi.nlm.nih.gov/pmc/articles/PMC3652533/

83 negativity bias: Rozin, P. & Royzman, E. (2001). Negativity bias, negativity dominance, and contagion. *Personality and Social Psychology Review.* 5(4), 296-320. Retrieved from http://www.wisebrain.org/media/Papers/NegativityBias.pdf

83 dress rehearse tragedy: OWN Network (Producer). (2013). *Brené brown breaks down common types of armor* [Video File]. Retrieved from http://www.oprah.com/oprahs-lifeclass/brene-brown-breaks-down-common-types-of-armor-video

84 gratitude journaling compared to other types of journaling... physical health benefits: Emmons, R. & McCullough, M. (2003). Counting blessings versus burdens: An experimental investigation of gratitude and subjective well-being in daily life. *Journal of Personality and Social Psychology.* 84(2), 377-389. Retrieved from http://psycnet.apa.org/doiLanding?doi=10.1037%2F0022-3514.84.2.377

84 emotional benefits correlated with gratitude: Wood, A., Froh, J. & Geraghty, A. (2010). Gratitude and well-being: A review and theoretical integration. *Clinical Psychology Review.* 30(7), 890-905. Retrieved from https://doi.org/10.1016/j.cpr.2010.03.005

84 gratitude can enhance our ability to relate with others: Harvard Health Publishing, (2011). *In praise of gratitude.* Retrieved from http://www.health.harvard.edu/newsletter_article/in-praise-of-gratitude

84 Interpersonal benefits associated with being more grateful: Wood et al., Gratitude and well-being: A review and theoretical integration. (see end note for page 84)

Chapter 8: Tools for Gratitude

95 The Gratitude Questionnaire: McCullough, M. *The gratitude questionnaire.* Retrieved from http://www.midss.org/content/gratitude-questionaire-gq-6

95 Greater Good's Gratitude Quiz: Greater Good Magazine. *Gratitude quiz.* Retrieved from http://greatergood.berkeley.edu/quizzes/take_quiz/6

96 "Give it Up" practice: Greater Good in Action. *Give it up.* Retrieved from http://ggia.berkeley.edu/practice/give_it_up

98 Gratitude HD - Moving Art: Schwartzberg, L. (2011). *Gratitude hd - moving art* [Video File]. Retrieved from https://www.youtube.com/watch?v=nj2ofrX7jAk

98 "Want to be happy? Be grateful": Steindl-Rast, D. (2013, Jun.). *Want to be happy? Be grateful* [Video File]. Retrieved from https://www.

END NOTES

ted.com/talks/david_steindl_rast_want_to_be_happy_be_grateful

98 Light a Candle: Gratefulness.org. *Light a candle.* Retrieved from http://gratefulness.org/light-a-candle/

99 Stop. Look. Go.: Gnarly Bay (Producer). *Stop. Look. Go.* [Video File]. Retrieved from http://gratefulness.org/resource/stop-look-go/

99 the three parts, as described on my own website: Lust, B. (2016). *Stop, look, go: A mindful gratitude practice from david steindl-rast.* Retrieved from https://learninglabconsulting.com/2016/10/31/stop-look-go-a-mindful-gratitude-practice-from-david-steidl-rast/

SECTION 3: GROWTH

Chapter 9: Introduction to Growth

107 "Please. Wake. Up": Watts, A. (1999). *The culture of counter-culture.* North Clarendon, VT: Tuttle Publishing.

111 that which is indestructible be found in us: Chödrön, P. (1996). *When things fall apart: Heart advice for difficult times.* Boulder, CO: Shambhala Publications.

111 Falling Upward: A Spirituality for the Two Halves of Life: Rohr, R. (2011). *Falling upward: A spirituality for the two halves of life.*

MYTHS OF BEING HUMAN

San Fransisco, CA: Jossey-Bass, a Wiley Imprint.

Chapter 10: The Path Toward Growth

113 Psychotherapist Tori Rodriguez describes this cultural shift: Rodriguez, T. (2013). *Negative emotions are key to well-being.* Retrieved from https://www.scientificamerican.com/article/negative-emotions-key-well-being/

114 difficult things... [become] the moment of truth: Graham, *Bouncing back: rewiring your brain for maximum resilience and well-being.* (see end note for page 36)

114–115 1. Opportunity . . . 5. Spiritual Growth/Depth: Tedeschi, R. & Calhoun, L. (2004). Posttraumatic growth: A new perspective on psychotraumatology. Retrieved from http://www.psychiatrictimes.com/ptsd/posttraumatic-growth-new-perspective-psychotraumatology-0

117 challenges release oxytocin: McGonigal, K. (2013, Jun.). *How to make stress your friend* [Video File]. Retrieved from https://www.ted.com/talks/kelly_mcgonigal_how_to_make_stress_your_friend

118 avoid thinking about white bears: Winerman, L. (2011). Suppressing the 'white bears': Meditation, mindfulness and other tools can help us avoid unwanted thoughts, says social psychologist daniel wegner. *Monitor on Psychology.* 42(9), 44. Retrieved from http://www.apa.org/monitor/2011/10/unwanted-thoughts.aspx

END NOTES

Chapter 11: Growth Practices

121 "The Personal Values Card Sort": Miller, W. R., C'de Baca, J., Mathews, D. B., & Wilbourne, P. L. (2001). *Personal values card sort.* Retrieved from http://www.motivationalinterviewing.org/sites/default/files/valuescardsort_0.pdf

126 On Being's webpage "The Poetry Radio Project": Krista Tippett Public Productions. *The poetry radio project.* Retrieved from https://onbeing.org/projects/poetry-radio-project/

128 photographs of Robert and Shana ParkeHarrison: Robert and shana parkeharrison. Retrieved from http://www.parkeharrison.com

130 Forgiveness is/taking the knife out your own back: Malik, H. (2016). *Raw.* (n.p.): Author.

Chapter 12: Tools for Growth

135 Post Traumatic Growth Inventory (PTGI): Calhoun, L.G. & Tedeschi, R.G. (2014). *Post traumatic growth inventory.* Retrieved from http://www.emdrhap.org/content/wp-content/uploads/2014/07/VIII-B_Post-Traumatic-Growth-Inventory.pdf

139 TEDTalk, Dweck: Dweck, C. (2014, Nov.). *The power of believing that you can improve* [Video File]. Retrieved from https://www.ted.com/

talks/carol_dweck_the_power_of_believing_that_you_can_improve

139 Mindset: The Psychology of Success: Dweck, C. (2007). *Mindset: The new psychology of success.* New York, NY: Ballantine Books

140 Grit: The power of passion and perseverance: Duckworth, A. (2013, Apr.). *Grit: The power of passion and perseverance* [Video File]. Retrieved from https://www.ted.com/talks/angela_lee_duckworth_grit_the_power_of_passion_and_perseverance

140 Angela Lee Duckworth on grit: Duckworth, A. (2016). *Grit: The power of passion and perseverance.* New York, NY: Scribner, An Imprint of Simon and Schuster, Inc.

140 grit scale: Duckworth, A. *Grit scale.* Retrieved from https://angeladuckworth.com/grit-scale/

140 grit is "passion and perseverance: Duckworth, *Grit: The power of passion and perseverance.* (see end note for page 140)

140 Bouncing Back: Rewiring Your Brain for Maximum Resilience: Graham, *Bouncing back: Rewiring your brain for maximum resilience and well-being.* (see end note for page 36)

141 "How To Make Stress Your Friend": McGonigal, *How to make stress your friend.* (see end note for page 117)

END NOTES

141 The Upside of Stress: Why Stress is Good for You, and How to Get Good At It: McGonigal, K. (2016). *The upside of stress: Why stress is good for you, and how to get good at it.* New York, NY: Avery, An Imprint of Penguin Random House LLC.

SECTION 4: CONNECTION

Chapter 13: Introduction to Connection

152 people who have power turn their story into a brick wall: Hannaham, J. (2015). *Delicious foods: A novel.* New York, NY: Little, Brown and Company.

Chapter 14: The Path Toward Connection

156 materialistic value orientation... people who operate from MVO: Kasser, T., Ryan, R, Couchman, C. & Sheldon, K. (2004). Materialistic values: Their causes and consequences. In T. Kasser and A. Kanner (Eds.), *Psychology and consumer culture: The struggle for a good life in a materialistic world.* Retrieved from https://www.researchgate. net/publication/232447683_Materialistic_values_Their_causes_ and_consequences

157 individuals were given an envelope of cash to donate to charity: Dunn, E., Aknin, L., & Norton, M. (2008). Spending money on others promotes happiness. *Science.* 319 (5870), 1687-1688. Retrieved from http://science.sciencemag.org/

content/319/5870/1687

157 charitable giving activates the reward center of the brain: Moll, J., Krueger, F., Zahn, R., Pardini, M., de Oliveira-Souza, R., Grafman, J. (2006). Human fronto-mesolimbic networks guide decisions about charitable donation. *Proceedings of the National Academy of Sciences in the United States of America.* 103(42), 15623-15628. Retrieved from http://www.pnas.org/content/103/42/15623.full.pdf

157 Connecting with others and showing compassion: Umberson, D. & Karas Montez, J. (2010). Social relationships and health: A flashpoint for health policy. *Journal of Health and Social Behavior.* 51(Suppl), S54-S66. Retrieved from https://www.ncbi.nlm.nih.gov/pmc/articles/PMC3150158/

157–158 a culture of "companionate love" is highly correlated with higher work satisfaction: Barsade, S. & O'Neill, O. A. (2014). What's love got to do with it?: A longitudinal study of the culture of companionate love and employee and client outcomes in a long-term care setting. *Administrative Science Quarterly.* 59(4), 551-598. Retrieved from https://www.researchgate.net/publication/267869088_What's_Love_Got_to_Do_with_It_A_Longitudinal_Study_of_the_Culture_of_Companionate_Love_and_Employee_and_Client_Outcomes_in_a_Long-term_Care_Setting

158 what our brains were wired for: reaching out and connecting with others: Cook, G. (2013). *Why we are wired to connect.*

Retrieved from https://www.scientificamerican.com/article/why-we-are-wired-to-connect/

158 social-cognitive and default mode networks (DMN) of the brain overlap in areas: Simmons, W. K., & Martin, A. (2012). Spontaneous resting-state bold fluctuations reveal persistent domain-specific neural networks. *Social Cognitive and Affective Neuroscience.* 7(4), 467-475. Retrieved from https://www.ncbi.nlm.nih.gov/pmc/articles/PMC3324567/

159 our interpersonal faculties . . . have supported our species' success: Zaki, J. & Ochsner, K. (2012). The neuroscience of empathy: Progress, pitfalls, and promise. *Nature Neuroscience.* 15(5), 675-680. Retrieved from https://doi.org/10.1038/nn.3085

160 lack of strong social connection has been linked to adverse health consequences: Seppälä, E. (2012). *Connect to thrive: Social connection improves health, well-being & longevity.* Retrieved from https://www.psychologytoday.com/blog/feeling-it/201208/connect-thrive

160 This worthiness . . . leads to deeper, more connected relationships: Brown, B. (2010, Jun.). *The power of vulnerability* [Video File]. Retrieved from https://www.ted.com/talks/brene_brown_on_vulnerability?language=en

160 We are biologically, cognitively, physically, and spiritually wired to love: Seppälä, *Connect to thrive: Social connection improves health,* *well-being & longevity.* (see end note for page 159)

Chapter 15: Connection Practices

172 quote from the novel The History of Love: Krauss, N. (2006). *The history of love.* New York, NY: W.W. Norton and Company.

176 Real Happiness: The Power of Meditation: Salzberg, *Real happiness: The power of meditation: A 28-day program.* (see end note for page 49)

Chapter 16: Tools for Connection

189 "The power of vulnerability": Brown, *The power of vulnerability.* (see end note for page 160)

190 "Listening to shame": Brown, B. (2012, Mar.). *Listening to shame* [Video File]. Retrieved from https://www.ted.com/talks/brene_brown_listening_to_shame

190 "5 ways to listen better": Treasure, J. (2011, Jul.). *5 ways to listen better* [Video File]. Retrieved from https://www.ted.com/talks/julian_treasure_5_ways_to_listen_better

191 Social: Why Our Brains Are Wired to Connect: Lieberman, M. (2013). *Social: Why our brains are wired to connect.* New York, NY: Crown Publishers, An Imprint of Random House.

END NOTES

CONCLUSION: CONNECTING WITH WHAT MATTERS

195 Sandberg and Grant pose a challenge: Tippett, K. (interviewer), Sandberg, S. & Grant, A. (interviewees). (2017). *Resilience after unimaginable loss.* Retrieved from https://onbeing.org/programs/sheryl-sandberg-and-adam-grant-resilience-after-unimaginable-loss/

195 How we spend our days is, of course, how we spend our lives: Tippett et al., *Resilience after unimaginable loss.* (see end note for page 195)

196 personal inadequacy, isolation, powerlessness, and loss of meaning . . . stress can have negative consequences: McGonigal, *The upside of stress: Why stress is good for you, and how to get good at it.* (see end note for page 141)

198 Personal Values Card Sort: Miller et al., *Personal values card sort.* (see end note for page 121)

203 Physical touch has been shown through research to have therapeutic benefits: Keltner, D. (2010). *Hands on research: The science of touch.* Retrieved from http://greatergood.berkeley.edu/article/item/hands_on_research

211 Goal-based intentions . . . Implementation intentions: Sheeran, P., Webb, T. & Gollwitzer, P. (2005). The interplay between goal intentions and implementation intentions. *Personality and Social*

Psychology Bulletin. 31(1), 87-98. Retrieved from http://www.psych. nyu.edu/gollwitzer/05_Sheeran_Webb_Gollwitzer_Goal_Intention_Implementation.pdf

212 attentional residue: Newport, C. (2016). *Deep work: Rules for focused success in a distracted world.* New York, NY: Grand Central Publishing.

216 create/a clearing/in the dense forest of your life: Postlethwaite, M. (2016). *Clearing.* Retrieved from https://frontiertherapymagazine.com/2016/12/14/clearing-a-poem-by-martha-postlewaite/